HOW IT ALL BEGAN IN YORKSHIRE

First published in Great Britain 1997 by
Dalesman Publishing Company Limited
Stable Courtyard, Broughton Hall
Skipton, North Yorkshire BD23 3AE
Reprinted 2000
Text © Maurice Baren

A British Library Cataloguing in Publication record
is available for this book

ISBN 1 85568 136 6

Colour Origination by Compass Reprographics
Printed by Midas Printing (HK) Limited

HOW IT ALL BEGAN IN YORKSHIRE

Maurice Baren

DEDICATION

I dedicate this book to all those who have helped me to appreciate the county of broad acres, of dales and moors and coast. To those, who from childhood, gave me an understanding of its cricket, its chapels and churches, its beautiful gardens and colourful characters, its legends, its good food – everything that makes Yorkshire great!

AUTHOR'S NOTE

I would like to thank those who have helped me in the compilation of this my fifth book. I am particularly grateful to those companies who have loaned me books, original material and illustrations – without such help the book could not have been produced. Many people have helped in a variety of ways and I hope I have thanked them all privately, but I would like publicly to acknowledge the help of the following: Elizabeth Stickney, the late Jack Allen, Derek Bamforth, Jimmy Corrigan and Tracey Corrigan-Clark, Billy Holdsworth, Barbara Ambler, the late Jack Crockatt, John Smallwood, Bill Mitchell, Margaret Waters, John Hudson, Michael Waddington, Simon Warner, Ernest Smith, Denis Greenwood, David Morrison, Philip Duxbury, Wakefield Metropolitan District Council, Kelvin Lawton, Mike England, Jane Oldroyd Hulme, Harrogate Council, M. G. Neesam, Leeds City Library and North Yorkshire County Library (Unné Collection), Mrs Connor, Mrs Greenalgh, Steve Kettlewell, Victor Watson, Tom Whiteley, David Wright, Louis Dobson, Dr Fred Kidd, Tom and Peggy Hewitt, Col E. W. Clay, B. W. Cookson, Ann Key and the staff of Dalesman Publishing Company. I am particularly grateful to fellow Yorkshireman and friend Alan Titchmarsh for providing the foreword.

I do apologise if I have failed to acknowledge the help of any other person. I would wish to assure them it is by accident and that I will gladly remedy it in future editions.

As with all my books, my wife Judith has been very much involved in its preparation. Her support in times of frustration and in times of discovery is really valued and I thank her for it.

CONTENTS

FOREWORD

I am a confirmed nosey parker. I can't help it. If I hear a word I've never heard before I have to look it up. If someone wants to know just what year the first man was sent up into space I have to find out there and then, even if it means leaving the table in the middle of dinner. (It was 1961 and his name was Yuri Gagarin.)

If the fact in question concerns Yorkshire then I am even more impatient to come up with the goods, and this book will thankfully save me hours of research. How Maurice Baren digs out this information I shall never know, though the fact that he was a gardener and trained in the same nursery as me probably has something to do with it. Maurice can dig up stories with a skill matched only by Howard Carter at the tomb of Tutankhamun.

Whether it is the inspiration behind those saucy seaside postcards, the Bamforth comics, or the origin of cat's eyes; the story of Wensleydale Cheese or the biography of Robert Thompson, the Mouseman of Kilburn, Maurice has a knack of wheedling out the facts and making you say 'gosh', just when you had taken the existence of all these things for granted.

I love a bit of Wensleydale Cheese with my fruitcake, and the oak chair I sit on to write this foreword has a mouse running up the leg, courtesy of Robert Thompson's craftsmen. I bought my first pair of hipsters from Greenwoods, and Rowntree's Fruit Pastilles were always stuffed in my pew when I was a choirboy at Ilkley Parish Church more years ago than I care to remember.

This book is something of a record of my life, but then it is a record of the life of everybody who has grown up in Yorkshire over the last fifty years. I can only hope you enjoy reading it as much as I have and that at the end, just as with a bit of fruitcake and cheese, you will want a little more.

ALAN TITCHMARSH

INTRODUCTION

Tykes, Yorkshire folk, are proud of their County; I am one of that number! Over the years many have worked hard to give it prosperity, and add not a little to their own pockets and those of their workers. We are known as a county of wool and steel, but Yorkshire business is about much more than that.

Some businesses, like the making of Wensleydale cheese, started as a craft developed by the farmer's wife in her own kitchen, but today, although still made in its local dale, it excites the taste buds of men and women in many parts of the world. Britain's fishing industry is only a shadow of what it was a century ago, but the Yorkshire coast continues to play an important part in the County's prosperity although companies such as J Marr of Hull have now diversified into other marine enterprises.

Did you know that 'Cat's Eyes' were the invention of a Yorkshireman and are still made in his home town; or that saucy picture postcards, sent home from Blackpool, Bournemouth or Bridlington, were created in Holmfirth; or that probably the world's largest supplier of fireworks is still based in Huddersfield? You might say it's a cat and mouse game, for on every piece of English oak furniture made in Kilburn, somewhere is a small carved mouse, perhaps climbing up the leg of a chair or down the side of a bookcase – a trade-mark known throughout the world.

Yorkshire is often described as a county of broad acres, each one seemingly different from the next. Yorkshire business is similarly varied and in this book I have tried to give a flavour of how Yorkshire folk make their 'brass', from selling linen or 'pop'; from making steel in the south of the county to training race horses in the north, from manufacturing textiles in the Pennines to building buses in Scarborough.

Yorkshire may be well-known for its love of cricket, brass bands and singing, but the stories of its business enterprise deserve to be equally well-known.

MAURICE BAREN

BIBLIOGRAPHY

A Fabric Huge by Mark Keighley 1989 Lister & Co

Plaxtons – Jubilee History

A Century in Progress – A Hundredth Birthday. Joshua Tetley & Son 1923

Quality Pays – The Story of Joshua Tetley & Son. Clifford Lackey, Springwood Books 1985

Robert Thompson – The Mouseman of Kilburn by James Thompson, Dalesman

Marr's – a centenary book

The History of Reckitt & Sons Ltd. Brian N. Reckitt 1958

Work Makes Wealth (Bradford and Bingley Building Society) by Tony Whiting 1989

Ups and Downs and Roundabouts by Joe Corrigan

Terry's of York 1767-1967

Racing Illustrated 1895

Various issues of Dalesman

A Century of Crockatt Cleaning. Crockatt Ltd 1975

Ogden (1893-1993) 100 years by Malcolm Neesam

Allens

William Grover Allen was born in Colchester, Essex, in 1855, the son of W F Allen, proprietor of a tailoring business. After attending the Colchester Grammar School he started work in the town and then 'travelled' for a well-known firm of outfitters.

He arrived in Harrogate as a youth in the days when High and Low Harrogate were separated by green fields and walkers passed through turnstiles to get from one to the other. High Harrogate was the fashionable part of town and there, in Regent Parade, William came to work for John Stokes, a tailor and outfitter. Later, when Stokes opened a shop in the elite James Street, William was appointed its manager, making a real success of the opportunity.

William married Emma Hiscoe and Charles William Hubert (Bert) Allen was born in 1879. The following year William Allen opened his own business in a lock-up shop in Parliament Street, but later had to move to premises on the other side of the street to make way for the building of the Royal Baths. At first he moved to 8 Parliament Street but later transferred to larger premises at 4 Parliament Street. In 1891, with financial help from his mother, he bought 6 Prospect Crescent for £2,530, probably a good bargain but not easy to afford; at that time many of the surrounding properties were still dwelling houses, very different from today!

Allen's shop in Parliament Street, Harrogate in the early 1880s

Working hours were long, the shop often being open to midnight on Saturday nights, for it was when the pubs closed that the menfolk proceeded to do their shopping; one can only imagine the harassment of the staff having to deal with customers who were rather inebriated.

The ground floor of the premises in Prospect Crescent consisted of the shop and cutting room, whilst down in the basement was a large workroom and stockroom. The first floor was sub-let to the Harrogate Coal Co., the second floor to the Crescent Athletic Club, and the third floor was leased to Mr Symington, a bookseller who had a shop in the market place.

Transportation in those early days was limited to a motorcycle with a bassinet trailer to accommodate the passenger. Mrs Allen only took one ride, and who can blame her, for it would 'chuff out' oil and petrol fumes and no doubt 'WG', to demonstrate his ability would go a little fast down a bumpy road or round a sharp corner, and then there would be the dust! It was quite a few years before he had a Jowett two seater, complete with hood and 'dicky seat'.

Mr Allen was very interested in the community in which he lived and worked and became honorary superintendent of the Harrogate Fire Brigade, one of the first serious fires he attended being at the Cairn Hydro (Hotel). He was also honorary superintendent of the Harrogate Volunteer Salvage Corps, for about 18 years a town councillor, captain of the Harrogate Cycle Club, a founder of the Pannal and Oakdale Golf Clubs, St John's Ambulance Association, and a staunch supporter of St. Peter's Church. Although he lost his first wife early in life, after having had five children, he married again and had a further three children. In 1922 he retired to Bournemouth and died there in 1931, at which time the Mayor of Harrogate said, "He always looked upon Mr Allen as one of the smartest men there were in the Borough."

When Bert Allen took over from his father he saw the potential in expanding the business and soon had three floors in operation. On the ground and lower ground floor was the ready-to-wear and shoe departments, on the first floor the boys' department, where for many years George Duffy reigned supreme. [Mr Duffy was a great character and the author remembers well, some fifty years later, how when his grandmother took him

Above, W G Allen was captain of the Harrogate Fire Brigade between 1889-1907; below left, the boys' and youths' department in the 1930s – thousands of young customers have ridden the rocking horse, including the author; below right, a typical 1980s Allens advertisement

to the shop for a suit, having tried a suit on, the young lad 'pulled a face' and Mr Duffy said "If he doesn't like it, he's not having it!"]

Over the years the business has been blessed by staff who have given a life-time of service to the firm. Albert Wilson joined Allen's as a jacket hand and became their alteration hand – such a title belies his importance in those days when so many children in the area attended public or grammar schools. School regulations would dictate more than one suit or blazer, and these garments would have to fit correctly, hence at certain times of the year the workroom would be very busy. Alteration hands were paid so much per alteration rather than a weekly wage and Albert would sit cross-legged on a bench, completely unruffled, but so often guiding sales staff out of difficulties, his needle always working! All tailors worked on Good Friday and it was the custom on that day to supply the workroom with rum and coffee – a tradition that both WG and Bert Allen respected.

Although Bert Allen was the head of the company his office was only a desk at the back of the boys' department, but nevertheless he encouraged the buyers to exercise their flair, thus attracting customers who wanted style, quality cloth and attention to detail. He strongly believed in the power of advertising which in those days was restricted to the local newspapers and to theatre programmes.

It is interesting to trace a typical day in the life of Bert Allen, similar to many others of that period. His business day would start at 9.30am with a browse through the correspondence, then a walk down to the Kiosk Cafe for a morning coffee and to meet many of the town's worthies. At midday it would be a short walk home for lunch, with a 'quickie' on the way; a short snooze and then back to the shop where at about 4.30pm he would leave for a pot of tea and buttered toast, before returning to work, until the shop closed

at 6.30pm. His day was not yet finished for now he would do the administrative work before joining his friends at the Crown Hotel for a game of billiards or snooker, before arriving home for supper between 9.30pm and 10 o'clock. Life may have been more relaxed in those days, it was the accepted way of life, but duties had to be done and the business made to succeed!

When WG died, Bert's sons Jack and Bill Allen were recalled from London to join the business; both served the company 'because it

The shop in Prospect Crescent during the early 1920s

was in their blood', working together for over 50 years. Theirs was an inborn heritage which had to be carried forward. Their goal was to make Allen's one of the finest shops in the north of England. The years of the Second World War were not easy ones in tailoring, with clothes on 'coupon', and in addition to this Bill Allen was called up to serve for six years in the forces. It was a battle to keep the business alive.

Today Allen's still maintains some of the grandeur of yesteryear with solid mahogany fittings and its sweeping staircase, giving it an air of indefinable quality, a rarity today. It is still a family business catering for Yorkshire families, but also as Jack and Bill dreamed, for people from across the whole of the north of England; those who still want quality and style.

ASDA

Although the name of ASDA may be known throughout Britain the company only came into being in 1965. However, several of the parts which came to create this large company have origins which date back to the early part of the century, and even beyond.

Milk pasteurisation was introduced at the end of the 19th century and this led to a need for more sophisticated equipment. To satisfy these needs farmers co-operated with one another to build milk factories. One such factory was built at West Marton, near Skipton, in 1900, to treat 500 gallons of milk a day. Arthur Stockdale had a milk wholesaling business in Grassington after the First World War, buying milk from farmers and sending it to dairies in Leeds. He joined with other local farmers under the name Hindell's Dairy Farmers Ltd, which was formed in 1920. The Craven Dairies Ltd, a subsidiary of Hindell's, the first to supply sterilized milk in the Leeds area, was also formed about this time. During the next 38 years Hindell's expanded considerably, opening 16 retail shops, several with cafes, in Leeds.

When Arthur Stockdale was on a skiing holi-day in Switzerland about this time he met Fred Zeigler, a German who had moved to live in England in 1899, and built up a number of pork shops. In 1928 Hindell's decided to diversify into selling pork products and set up a shop at 118 Kirkgate, Leeds; it was an instant success and a subsidiary company, Farm Stores Ltd, was formed with Fred Zeigler as a major share holder. Gradually more shops were added and the range of products extended to include such items as black puddings, roast pork, pies and sausage rolls. Eventually the directors bought a meat processing factory; by 1937 there were 15 Farm Store shops.

In 1936 Bramhams (Foods) Ltd was founded; they had a bakery in Dixon Lane, Wortley, a shop in Bradford and three in Leeds. They developed a large wholesale trade in hams and pies.

One company, bought for investment purposes, which did not seem to fit this portfolio, was the Newthorpe Lime Works Ltd, at Sherburn-in-Elmet, which was acquired in 1942.

Associated Dairies and Farm Stores (Leeds) was incorporated as a public company in 1949, to acquire the share capital of Hindell's Dairy Farmers Ltd. It consisted of nine operating companies with interests as diverse as bakers, cafe proprietors, pork butchers, bacon curers, retailers, farmers and milk businesses in Yorkshire, Durham and Northumberland. They had eight dairies, two bakeries, forty-two shops, farms totalling 3,500 acres, over 200 vehicles and 1,200 staff. Arthur Stockdale became managing director.

Other companies acquired in subsequent years included

ASDA's first Welsh outlet, at Newport, as seen in the 1970s with parking for up to 900 cars

Northern Dairies (Sunderland) Ltd, West Riding Dairy Farmers Ltd and Provincial Dairies Ltd of Leeds and Harrogate. This latter company was formed in 1874 and had premises in Park Lane and Upperhead Row, just off Briggate. The shop at 37 Upperhead Row was of a very high standard with marble and carved oak panels (with artistic representations of cows, poultry, etc.) and marble topped counters. Each week, in the 1890s, they were selling 7,000 gallons of milk, five hundredweights of butter, 300 quarts of cream, and 2,000-3,000 fresh eggs; they employed sixty to seventy staff. They supplied 'pure new milk and nursery milk twice daily', and churned much of their own butter.

Chairman in the 1970s,
A N Stockdale

In 1963 the company's name was shortened to Associated Dairies Ltd.

Peter and Fred Asquith came from a family of Yorkshire butchers. In Castleford, the Queen's Theatre had been turned into a bingo hall, but in the 1960s they converted it into their first supermarket. It needed a new floor but they laid this themselves; they filled the shelves themselves with branded goods, but cut the prices. In 1965 resale price maintenance, which meant that the manufacturer could determine what price a product sold at, was still in force, but they ignored the set prices. In store-opening newspaper advertisements in 1963 they proclaimed 'Permanent Reductions' and also announced that the store was open until 8pm on Fridays – late night shopping and regular low prices had arrived. They opened a further store at Edlington in South Yorkshire.

Peter Asquith had been discussing with Associated Dairies the possibilities of them running the fresh food and meat concessions in his supermarkets. This led to a meeting with Arthur Stockdale's son, Noel, who was vice chairman, and Eric Binns, managing director of Associated Dairies. Noel was very impressed with Peter Asquith and the supermarkets, but also had a vision of Associated Dairies' future in this area. He convinced his board and on 3rd May 1965 the Asquiths sold their interests to Associated Dairies and a new company Asda Stores Ltd. was formed with Fred and Peter Asquith as the joint managing directors.

ASDA came about when the Asquith brothers joined with Noel Stockdale to bring the two companies together. There is still debate on how the name 'ASDA' came into being – it might be that the 'AS' comes from Asquith, but more likely that 'AS' came from Associated and 'DA' from Dairies.

In September 1965 ASDA opened its first new store, at South Elmsall, near Wakefield. At the side of the supermarket was an enormous car park – the era of 'park and shop' had been born. Again the shelves were stocked with well known branded goods, but at much lower prices than in other shops.

Within a month Wakefield had its own new store – the new company was on its way forward as other stores at Whitkirk, Billingham and Halifax quickly opened.

Another early acquisition was the GEM superstore in Nottingham, bought from Gem International of America; with a floor area of 80,000 square feet and car parking for 1,000 cars – it was twenty times bigger than their Castleford store. By 1970, now with over 30 stores, only a third of the floor space was used for food sales, the remainder was used to display household goods – one stop shopping had arrived!

ASDA's move south came in 1977 when they built the store at South Woodham Ferers, Chelmsford. In the early years low prices for well known brands had been all important; now another factor was added – the stores must also look good! A local authority suggested that a superstore had a roof like an aircraft hangar – ASDA's response was to call in an architectural partnership to design a roof made of handmade tiles cast from Essex clay. The store later won awards for its design!

The 1980s saw the company look increasingly to staff training and to making the stores more 'user friendly'. Restaurants were introduced into stores and changing facilities were provided for mums with babies. ASDA own brand goods were only introduced in 1986. Other develop-

The Associated Dairies Group

ments before the end of the decade were the introduction of the 'George' range of designer clothes, items designed by George Davies, the founder of Next shops, and the acquisition of the Gateway chain with its 61 supermarkets.

However during the 70s and 80s the company also diversified into estate agencies with Asda Property Shop, car sales with Asdadrive, and acquired other non-core businesses; these proved to be unfortunate departures from its central focus and have been disposed of. During this period there were also board room disagreements and these, and the effects of 1988 'Black Monday', caused the company serious financial problems.

It wasn't until December 1991 that a new vision came, with the arrival of Archie Norman as Chief Executive. He came with an excellent track record and quickly set about re-focusing the company. To gain financial stability he imposed a pay freeze across the company and made an emergency rights issue of £350 million. To secure a positive attitude within the company he broke down barriers between headquarters and stores and brought in internal competition, encouraging staff to be one team. In the stores changes had to take place to make them more 'customer friendly', which meant a complete physical redesign; more own brand products were introduced. Layers of management were also removed and with the impact of computerised stock control efficiencies came into being.

Within a year a £1 billion debt mountain had been reduced to £76 million and sales volumes were up by 27%. Archie Norman had achieved the impossible! Customers were returning to ASDA. Today with sales of over £6 billion, operating profits of £313 million, and with six million customers shopping at Asda each week, the company is now in a very strong position. In the 1997 General Election Archie Norman became the Conservative MP for Tunbridge Wells. Allan Leighton is now the chief executive officer at ASDA.

Bamforth

& Co Ltd

The Bamforths were painters and decorators in Holmfirth in the 1840s, and a decade or so later, when James Bamforth left school, he went to work with the family firm. He was an artistic lad with a great interest in photography and a flair for painting scenic backcloths at great speed. Soon he was using his skills to paint backcloths for scenes for the lantern-slides the firm made to take around neighbouring village halls, in the days before the cinema.

James Bamforth had five sons and two daughters; Edwin was the businessman whilst Harry went to New York to open up an office for the developing company. Sister Janey helped with the props and dressed up the local people who became the 'stars' of the lantern shows.

By 1870 Bamforth was established in Holmfirth and very soon they had an extensive range of lantern-slides, often relating to the story behind a popular song of the day, or perhaps a well-loved hymn.

About the turn of the century the picture-postcard started to become popular and from the lantern slides they created sentimental postcards, often depicting one verse of a song or hymn, thus making sets of three, four or five cards. It was also in those pre-First World War years that Bamforth's made many silent movie films, some of these being sent overseas to countries as far away as Russia. When the weather was inclement these novice film makers shot their films on indoor sets, with their handpainted backgrounds; when the story called for a bankraid then Edwin Bamforth would arrange with the local bank manager for the company to 'borrow' the bank for a few hours while the appropriate scenes were shot, and often the locals would be the 'extras', chasing the 'raiders' down the main street!

While Charlie Chaplin, Douglas Fairbanks and Mary Pickford became international stars, local actors such as Bertie Wright, Lily Ward and Fred Beaumont were glad they had kept their day jobs! Bamforth's made their silent films – being silent meant there were no language barriers – from 1899-1915.

Throughout the years that Bamforth's have produced postcards they have always made a wide range of cards portraying views of popular holiday resorts, and also greetings cards, but it was following the First World War when sentimental cards had lost their appeal, that they

I could have sweared I saw a torpedo.

You've got to keep your end up to be in the swim at MORECAMBE

Above, one in the 'Topical Kids' series produced in the early years of the century; right, some cards were superimposed with a resort's name, this one from the 1920s

started producing the comic postcard. One of their first artists was Douglas Tempest, but for over 50 years Arnold Taylor has been chief artist and has produced many of the original designs. They also employed freelance artists who would perhaps submit 100 drawings, and have only a third accepted for publication.

As working-class people went year after year for their annual one week's holiday to a favoured resort such as Blackpool or Scarborough, they would get tired of sending a limited range of views and so enjoyed picking an appropriate comic, often risque card for a certain sister or for their workmates at the mill. Such cards probably reached their peak demand during the 1930s to the 1970s, when Bamforth's were selling 20 million cards a year. At that time they were producing 4,000 different view cards; 100 new comic cards were produced each year, with the 50 best sellers from previous years being retained as stock items. Cards depicting the henpecked husband and domineering wife and the cheeky, spicy cards had become a British institution! Ninety per cent of their comic postcards were sold at the seaside.

It was important to ensure that the postcards were always topical. When radio was just becoming popular then the catchphrase and the drawing would relate to that; when television came along the card would poke

A LITTLE BIT OF HEAVEN (1)
Have you ever heard the story of how Ireland got its name?
I'll tell you so you'll understand from whence old Ireland came;
No wonder that we're proud of that dear land across the sea,
For here's the way me dear old mother told the tale to me.

A card in the 'Songs' series — often three or four cards were needed, each with one verse on it

fun at a particular programme or where the TV was sited. The cards were designed to be amusing but not offensive and many cards received the 'blue pencil', before they reached the printing stage.

In 1936 young Derek Bamforth returned home, having been away at school, but by now his father was ill and on Edwin's death he took over the running of the business although he was only 18 years old. However he soon had to leave the business again when he joined the territorial army.

After the Second World War sales continued to boom although in latter years, with more risque programmes on television, people were less likely to be shocked as programmes brought a wider view of life into the home and from then on there was a decline in interest in the saucy postcard.

In 1987 Derek felt ready to retire and Bamforth & Co Ltd was sold to E T W Dennis & Sons Ltd, Scarborough. Although Bamforth cards are still produced, it is no longer in the town of their birth.

"HOW MUCH ARE THE NEW-LAID EGGS?"
"TWOPENCE EACH. YOU CAN HAVE THE CRACKED ONE FOR A PENNY!"
"CRACK ME A DOZEN THEN, WILL YE!"

Left, an early card by Arnold Taylor who was chief artist for more than 50 years

BEN SHAWS

– SINCE 1871 –

Benjamin Shaw was born in 1837, at Fenay Bridge, on the outskirts of Huddersfield. His father was a farm labourer, but often there was no work and Ben could only go to school when his father had a job. He left school when he was 13 and learned to be a spinner, one of the most skilled jobs in the woollen industry, but still badly paid in the hard days of the mid-1800s. Eventually he became manager of a spinning co-operative.

However Huddersfield was one of those fast developing towns which had recently become a Borough, commerce and industry were increasing at a pace, and Ben, a striking bearded figure in his mid-thirties, along with his brother George, decided to leave textiles and start out on their own.

In 1871 they formed 'Shaw Bros., Manufacturers of Non-Alcoholic Beverages'. It is likely that they had little knowledge of their new trade for there is a

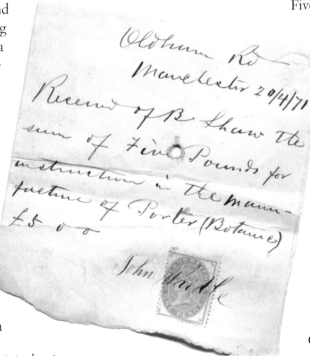

receipt for £5 made out by John Wardle of Manchester for 'instruction in the manufacture of Porter (Botanic)'. Originally a porter was a cheap beer made for labourers, but theirs was a very different product being composed of herbs, and of course it was non-alcoholic. They also made ginger beer, brewed according to an old family recipe. It is said the ginger beer was matured in old spirit barrels, which no doubt gave it a little extra taste!

Soon Ben was to be seen trundling his flat-bottomed wheelbarrow, with its load of bottles, as he made his first delivery to Thornton's, a famous temperance hotel in the town where many of the teetotal radicals met.

Within a month of starting the business they upgraded their transport arrangements; they bought, again from John Wardle, a cart and harness for £6, paying £3 down and agreeing to pay the balance in four months time, such was their tight budget.

Five years after the partnership had been formed, it was dissolved and Ben paid out to his brother £317. 13s 6d. Ben had been the inspiration of the business, now he was the sole owner. He was a man respected for his character, independence and enterprise, and he was determined to succeed.

The first 'manufactory' was in Elms Yard, in Charles Street, Huddersfield, but twelve years later he moved to a sub-

Right, the receipt for the original recipe,
which Ben Shaw bought for £5

Right, the opening page in Benjamin Shaw's Almanack for 1892;
below an advertisement from the Almanack

stantial three-storey building, 1-5 Upperhead Row, at Westgate Corner. Within a decade this also became too small and this time he leased a large plot of land in Willow Lane, close to Bay Hall, and built 'one of the finest mineral water manufactories in the Kingdom'. He gave details of this move in his 'Almanac for 1892', of which he published 10,000 copies at 1d each, also informing his customers that he would be keeping a 'Town Office', for their convenience. He also told them that when orders were received they would be 'telephoned to the works immediately'; he was one of the pioneers of this particular use of the telephone.

Ben's first registered trademark was a dandelion plant, indicating that his drinks were based on natural herbs and roots, but as his range of products extended he registered a new trade mark, 'Benjamin Shaw, Amicus Humani Generis', which means 'Benjamin Shaw, friend of the human race'!

'Non-alcoholic Beverages' was a term used to attract the 'teetotal' trade, although some of the early non-licensed drinks were brewed, and one suspects that those who drank 'Ben's Botanic Porter', 'Dandelion Stout' or 'Horehound Beer' did not question the term too closely when the actual drinks pleased their palates so much.

Brewed drinks gradually declined in the 19th century as sparkling drinks such as Lemonade, Orangeade and Aerated Lime Juice appeared in his list. 'Mineral Waters' became another important section, these being manufactured equivalents of waters which flowed from natural springs; popular among these were Potass Water, Lithia Water, Seltzer Water and Soda Water, the latter being the only one sold today. Cordials were another feature of his lists and claimed to be 'prepared from fresh fruit'; they included Raspberry, Peppermint, Lime Juice and Gingerette. 'Hop Ale' was another distinctive drink, its popularity lasting some 50 years; it was fermented in large tanks made of slate and was the ideal answer for those who had a palate for beer but an abstainer's conscience! It was a very pleasant drink, more 'hoppy' than 'malty', but when the customs and excise put a tax on any product using the word beer or ale this badly affected sales.

But to many people the accepted name for a fizzy drink was 'pop'. The authentic pop bottle was the one with the indented neck and captive glass ball, which was sealed against a rubber ring by pressure from the fizzy contents. Early bottles of this nature were called 'Codd's' after their inventor, and it is said that the term 'Codswallop' came from this, the 'wallop' referring to the drink in them (which may have had a slight alcoholic content at that time).

Ben Shaw always realised the importance of his water supplies and when he built the Willow Lane factory he had a water main specially laid so that he could use water from the Pennines which had proved so palatable at his Upperhead Row site. From the main the water passed through 'pure block tin' pipes, then through a 'patent rectifier' and a 'powerful filter' before being refrigerated; this was one hundred years ago!

Above and left, the modern face of Ben Shaw's

During the first half of the 20th century many of the deliveries were by horse-drawn transport with waggons piled high, but with the passing years and the move to mechanised fleets, now one vehicle may be carrying more than 20 tons of drink down the motorway system.

Today the glass bottle has been largely replaced by the plastic one or by the can. The can was first used as a container for soft drinks in the United States in the early part of the 1950s, but in 1958 the Metal Box Company contacted Ben Shaw's and experimental work began. In 1959 Ben Shaw's introduced cans into the market place, the first independent manufacturer in Europe to do so.

Today the original factory produces over 40 million litres of Spring Water a year. This is drawn from the borehole which was sunk in the 1930s and sourced from the finest spring water which has permeated through the Pennines for over sixty years. The company has also developed into the third largest soft drinks dispensing company in Great Britain and is now a member of the Rutland Trust PLC who continue to support and invest in the development of Ben Shaw & Sons.

Ben Shaw had great foresight when he chose the site for his first factory – one with a fine source of spring water.

JOHN FOSTER

(BLACK DYKE MILLS)

The first days of John Foster, who was born in 1798, and his Queensbury venture are unfortunately lost in the mists of time. We know that in 1819 he married Ruth Briggs and started as a worsted manufacturer. His father was a colliery owner and farmed at Thornton near Bradford, while his father-in-law was a land owner in Queensbury.

The bleak moorland village of Queensbury, high above Bradford but only a few miles from Keighley, Halifax, Huddersfield, all centres for the worsted trade, and quite near to Burnley where other textiles, mostly cotton, were

produced. The hand-loom weavers he employed in those early days would live in isolated cottages around the area, 'eking out' a living by working at home. In those early days the weavers were producing damasks and lastings; the latter were hard wearing cloths as their name suggests.

We do not know if either of the fathers helped to finance the new venture, or whether it was the buoyant state of the industry in 1818 which encouraged John Foster to embark on such an enterprise. If it was the latter he might have been dismayed soon afterwards for the next two years were times of depression. By 1827 he was doing well and was prosperous enough to build Prospect House which remained his home until he retired to live at Hornby Castle.

At that time his business could be divided into three areas; the worsted, weaving and spinning was the most important, but he was also a partner in a colliery as well as having a shop. Each was interlinked and all played a part in the system by which his hundred or so hand loom weavers were 'paid' – often receiving goods from the shop or colliery in exchange for work done.

John Foster would buy yarn and distribute it from a warehouse at the back of Prospect House, at the junction of the Keighley-Brighouse and Bradford-Halifax roads, to the hand-loom weavers who then brought in their woven pieces. John took these pieces to the Bradford Piece Hall to sell to merchants who would arrange for the dyeing and finishing.

In 1828 he rented Cannon Mill for spinning, prior to

Centre, John Foster; above a general view of the Queensbury mills from the south east as it looked in 1949

erecting the first part of Black Dyke Mills in 1835. In 1834 John's father-in-law conveyed part of some land known as Black Myres to him and here he started to build his mill. Black Dykes Farm, from which the mill gets its name, wasn't passed to him until 1842.

By 1835 John Foster was employing 700 hand-loom weavers but to bring some of these people – for he kept a mix of factory and hand-loom work-ers – into a mill environment was something of a problem, for the Factories Act had just been passed, which regulated working hours and ages of employees. There were, however, only four inspectors to cover the whole of the country!

As power looms were introduced, mills prolif-erated where good levels of coal existed locally. It took only ten months, from the cutting of the first sod to the spindles starting to turn at Black Dyke Mills – by February 1838 he had spent over £9,000 on this first stage of the mill, including its machinery and fittings! In 1835, with between 3-4,000 spindles working, he produced about 6,000 lbs of yarn a week; over the next 50 years that figure would multiply ten times.

Worsted manufacturing was in the hands of a small number of big employers and they either already had, or found it easier to raise, capital for such mill building projects. As John Foster saw his profits increase he ploughed money back into further extensions; in 1836 a gas works was erected which served both the mill and the village; by 1843 the weaving shed had 500 looms.

By 1851 Black Dyke Mills was dominating the landscape and at the Great Exhibition John Foster took first prize for alpaca, which he had been experimenting with since 1837, and for mohair fabrics, and the gold medal for yarns.

The physical development of the mill itself followed the technological advances taking place in textile production. In 1874 dyeing and soap making were added to the processes carried out at the mill; in 1890 a plush works was also added

(plush material used for furnishings was made from mohair). After this date little change took place to the mill's shape and size. The total floor area of the mill covered about 15 acres. Already they were exporting to many countries includ-ing Germany, Russia, Italy, North and South America, and Australasia.

The Foster family was blessed with many sons; John and Ruth had six, who all became involved in the business. The oldest son, William, born in 1821, was already involved in the business by 1835 and did not retire until 1882. He

The group drive combing section

was six years older than his next brother and having been involved in the company from such a young age this put him into a dominant posi-tion in the hierarchy of the business – indeed the company remained John Foster & Son Ltd, not Sons! He was made a partner in 1842 and it was William's sons who took control in 1884 fol-lowing John Foster's death.

William married twice and had thirteen chil-dren. He was a man of influence in the social life of the community and no doubt the Black Dyke Mills Band played its part when he entertained guests or business acquaintances in the style of the time. A brass reed band had been founded in Queensbury in 1815 but when its survival was under threat John Foster invited them to become

*The Black Dyke Mills Band
winners of the cherished Daily
Herald National Championship
Trophy (below) three times
during the 1940s*

associated with Black Dyke Mills. By 1855 the band had 19 musicians, most of them from Queensbury or workers at the mill. The band has been national champions 16 times in the last 50 years and British Open Champions 26 times. As early as 1906 it toured Canada and in 1993 was the first British brass band to perform at New York's Carnegie Hall.

In 1891 the firm became a limited liability company, but it was not until 1948 that the company was floated on the stock exchange. The same year the directors erected the Victoria Hall in Queensbury for the benefit of its workers and the local community – it had a concert hall with gallery to seat 650 people, library, billiard room and many other facilities. Adjoining the concert hall was built a large swimming bath with facilities in the basement for people to wash clothes; all the heat was provided by steam from the Black Dyke Mills and the construction of the hall and baths was carried out by the company's workmen.

In the 20th century John Foster & Son Ltd knew troubled times as markets and demands changed and the country became embroiled in two world wars and a major economic depression. Labour patterns changed as households had smaller families and Bradford's new businesses drew labour away from Queensbury. A hostel was built to house 231 beds for girls who faced unemployment in the north east after the First World War, and following the Second World War this was reopened and one for boys was also opened, but still there was a lack of labour and some machinery remained idle. So a factory was built in Cumnock in Ayrshire where labour was available and some of the machinery was moved to that town.

The imposition of import tariffs by the United States in the early 1960s killed many business opportunities and Black Dyke Mills looked to Japan and started travelling within that country. A considerable business was built up and this is still maintained. Over the years the company has acquired several local independent textile companies and recently other companies, often not related to the textiles, have become tenants or bought areas within the mill complex, creating a thriving business community.

With the decline of the British textile industry John Foster & Son may be operating to a lower capacity but it is involved in producing high quality luxury suiting for export; about 75% of production is exported. Additionally 25% of its business is still in the production of mohair materials, carrying on a tradition stretching back 150 years.

BRADFORD & BINGLEY
BUILDING SOCIETY

Bradford and Bingley, although geographically close, were and are different in many ways. However, two building societies, formed in the same year, have come together and become a national leader. The earliest Bradford building society was the Bradford Union Building Society founded in 1825, followed by the Bradford Second Equitable Benefit Building Society formed in 1851. It is the Bradford Second Equitable which spawned the modern Society.

The 1850s were prosperous in Bradford with such influential names as Semon, Illingworth, Lister, Cheesborough and Salt already established in textiles. The town was now seeing its horizons widening in its world-wide export trade.

On 18 August 1851 at the first subscription meeting prospective members were told that shares would be £120 each, members to pay a subscription of 10s a month for 13 years, 10 months and six days. The Society was to be 'permanent', as opposed to a terminal society, one generally wound up when the money needed to build the scheme was achieved. In the first year the Society had 557 members, 503 investing shareholders, 54 borrowers. The income

was £11,000 and £9,000 was advanced on mortgages – and all the result of an advertising campaign which cost £3 14s 10d! The interest paid on deposits was 4%, and on unadvanced shares 5%.

The Society's first mortgage went to John Abbey, a weaving overlooker who moved from Halifax to Bradford; his house, at 11 Clayton Lane, needed to be large as there were seven in the family – he needed £300 to buy the property and had mortgage repayments of £2. 10s 0d a month.

During those early years the Society lent money on shops, chapels, Sunday schools, workshops, warehouses and mills, as well as on houses. Bradford was growing rapidly and large numbers of houses were being built.

First year results moved the delighted directors to double the salaries of the Society's officers. However, 1854 was a bad year for many financial institutions due to trade depression, and many members withdrew investments and emigrated to Australia or America. That year the Society experienced its first cash flow crisis, and a group of directors 'waited upon' their bank manager to negotiate a £1,000 overdraft.

When the old Society was wound up in 1858 the Bradford Equitable rented rooms in Darley Street for £12 per year, including light and heat. Gradually the working classes gained confidence in the Society as a way of saving. Every Friday evening the Society's meeting rooms would be opened to receive members' subscriptions and to collect depositors' funds. In 1880 the Society earned a profit of £42,063.

The Building Societies Association held its annual

The coats of arms for Bradford Equitable (right) and Bingley (left) were both incorporated into the coat of arms for the Bradford and Bingley (Page 26)

meeting in Bradford in 1898, the year after Bradford became a city. By 1900 slum clearance had begun in Bradford and the building of back-to-back houses ceased. The Society prospered – in 1911 they installed a telephone and purchased a brief-size typewriter; in 1912 the Society's assets exceeded £1 million.

During the First World War the Society loaned large sums of money to the government, but at the end was in a strong position, and in 1920 opened offices in Bank Street. In 1926 it was suggested that the Society appoint an agent in Coventry, but this was turned down because one of the directors felt that motor cars would not last!

Secondary school leaver Teasdale Walter James joined the Society in 1922 and eventually became personal assistant to the secretary and manager. A man of vision, in 1936 he was sent to London to work alongside the manager as the director's representative; later greater responsibilities would be entrusted to him.

During the Second World War the Society became an official agent for the sale of National Savings Certificates and Defence Bonds and by the end of the war its assets exceeded £10 million. The Society expanded nationally opening branches in Manchester, Glasgow and other major cities.

In 1946, after further mergers, the Society became the Bradford Equitable Building Society. Winston Churchill led the Conservatives to power in 1951 and they set a target to build 300,000 houses a year, stressing the value of home ownership. This was also the Society's centenary year; by now they had assets of £22 million.

Towards the end of the 1950s Francis Lumb retired after twenty years as senior executive and was replaced, as general manager, by Walter James. Two years later Burroughs machine posting equipment was introduced. The Society saw much growth after Walter James' appointment; in 1962 he was appointed a director.

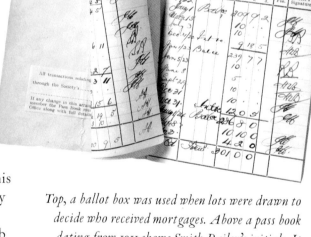

Top, a ballot box was used when lots were drawn to decide who received mortgages. Above a pass book dating from 1911 shows Smith Bailey's initials. It originally belonged to the father of Frank Sutcliffe, a member of staff from 1928 to 1975 and London manager from 1934 to 1962

Meanwhile a parallel operation had been developing in nearby Bingley, a town dramatically changed by the Industrial Revolution. Workers there had created friendly societies, forerunners of the Bingley Building Society.

A terminating building society was set up in Bingley in 1807, when the town had a population of 3,000, but it was almost half a century later before the first permanent building society, The Bingley, Morton and Shipley Permanent Benefit Building Society was formed. At the end of its first year it had an income of £5014, and had advanced £4718 to 9 members.

In 1864 Nicholas Walbank was appointed secretary, a post he held for 40 years. In the period up to 1876, 46 new streets were laid out in Bingley; and Titus Salt was building his industrial model village, in nearby Saltaire. The 1880s were years of depression and it was not until the 1890s that growth was re-established. Now the Society bought its own offices, two converted houses in Queen Street, Bingley. In 1899 Smith Bailey was appointed treasurer; five years later he became secretary, a post he held for 35 years, after which he was appointed a director.

Even after the end of the First World War it was still policy to have two directors sign each cheque and a young clerk would trudge from company to company for the required signatures. The Society must have had the oldest group of directors on record, for the five members of the board had a collective age of 399 years, three of them being in their 80s!

In 1929 the Society became the Bingley Building Society and soon had assets of £3 million with collection points in several northern towns and cities. In 1932 the president told his members "Today we are amongst the leading societies in the country", but it was still the age of heavy ledgers and high stools. In 1934 a London office opened in Kingsway. By 1951, the Bingley Building Society's centenary year, assets had risen to over £17 million. In 1959, after 45 years service, Raymond Bailey retired, to be succeeded by Robert T Gardner, at 35 the youngest chief executive of any society.

After a meeting of the Yorkshire County Association of Building Societies in 1963, Walter James confided to Bob Gardner his intention to retire. He said he would like him to be his successor; Bob however suggested that it would be more sensible for the Societies to merge. The Bingley would not consider a takeover, but would merge providing there was parity on the board with the two general managers working jointly until the retirement of Walter James in 1966. It was agreed

The first floor offices of the society's Bank Street premises occupied in 1895; below, a 1934 advertisement from the Yorkshire Observer

that the partnership would be called the Bradford & Bingley Building Society, with its head office in Main Street, Bingley. The two Societies had much in common; the Bradford had assets of £56million, the Bingley £46million; the Bradford had 23 branches, the Bingley 29. In 1963 when the merger was made public, the Bradford was 13th in the table of largest societies and the Bingley 17th; the merger made the Bradford & Bingley the 8th largest society with assets of over £100million. The Bradford & Bingley Building Society opened officially on 1 July 1964. A new Coat of Arms, incorporating the crests of the Societies, was granted in August 1964.

Bob Gardner and Walter James had tremendous enthusiasm for the new Society which they conveyed to their staff with great vigour. For months the staff worked from nine in the morning until nine at night, and through weekends, to build a first division building society. New policies had to be developed, but the objectives of the Society were the same as those of the founding societies of 1851, to encourage thrift and offer security to investors and also 'to the great benefit to the national economy, to enable those who, with great pride and satisfaction to themselves and their families, wish to enjoy their very own plot in this great country of ours.'

Advertising campaigns exploited the concept of bees, picking up the Bs of the Bradford & Bingley. When Walter James retired, Bob Gardner became sole general manager. In 1967 the Society lent a record £37million, a 16% increase on the previous year; total assets had now reached £178mil-

A secure home for your money.

Bigger than ever this year. Mr. Bradford

...and better than ever. Mr. Bingley

lion. That year the National Housebuilders Registration Council was formed, giving new homeowners many safeguards.

The Option Mortgage Scheme gave new benefits to home-owners on low incomes; Save As You Earn came in 1969, and decimalisation of coinage in 1971 brought extra work-loads. 1973 was a boom time, work started on a new head office and the Society broke through the £500million asset landmark.

By 1974 its new £2.5million head office was complete; it was large, impressive, modern in design and built of stone to convey solidarity and permanence, but always controversial! The public's awareness of the Society increased with television advertising, using the now famous Mr Bradford and Mr Bingley campaign.

In 1984 Bob Gardner's work was acknowledged when he was awarded the CBE. It marked the end of a great career but he later served the Society as president. He was succeeded by Geoffrey Lister, who had joined the Society in 1965, who became chief executive. During his period of office 30 smaller mergers took place, which helped its assets to rise from £4 billion to £16 billion, and made it truly a national mutual society.

The Society needed again to expand its head office in 1992 and a further building was opened at Crossflatts, near Bingley. In 1996 Christopher Rodriques became chief executive on the retirement of Geoffrey Lister. The Bradford & Bingley Building Society, still a mutual organisation, in 1997 was the 2nd largest mutual building society with assets of over £18 billion.

DAVID BROWN
G R O U P P L C

David Brown was born into humble surroundings in Huddersfield about 1843. At that time the town had terrible slums, the living conditions of workers were grim, hours were long and wages were bad. Young David Brown, only 5 feet 3 inches in height, was interested in neither church nor politics – his religion was work!

At the age of 17 he started making wooden patterns, in a stable belonging to his landlord Thomas Broadbent, who also had a foundry. To begin with 'Brown and Broadbent' was a partnership, and from this work David gradually built up capital to start a business in which initially he employed two men to work with him. By 1873 he had moved to larger premises, in nearby Chapel Street, and extended his work to include the 'manufacture of all kinds of Spur, Skew, Bevel and Eccentric gear', a vital step for the future. However, he had to use other local foundries for he had no foundry of his own.

In 1879 he turned his firm into a limited company, David Brown & Company, with the registered office at his home, 72 South Street, Huddersfield, where he lived for the next 30 years. In the early 1880s he started 'cogging mortise wheels' – inserting wooden cogs into mortised cast iron wheel rims, which were held in position by wedges. An innovation of the time, which was of significance to David Brown,

David Brown who founded the firm at the age of 17

was the development of the 'involute', the curved shape of the gear teeth, which greatly improved the consistent running of the gears. By 1890 the company only employed ten people, including David's two sons, Ernest and Frank; the youngest son, Percy, brought their breakfast at 8.30am each day before he went to school. David and his sons started work at 6.15am – one of them had to open up the works, for no one else was allowed to have a key; all would work a 53 hour week.

About 1895 the works were destroyed by fire and around that time David Brown had a serious accident severing his thumb and damaging his hand. After the fire the Browns built a three-storied building in East Parade and as the business prospered they employed about 150 pattern makers, but Ernest and Frank saw the future in the manufacture of machine cut gears. Their first gear cutters were imported from America and Germany. However production was not easy, for often holes would be found when machining the castings and the wheel would have to be scrapped.

It was realised that even if David Brown & Company became the largest pattern maker in Britain it would only employ about 200 men; the sons saw that the future was in machine cut gears. Father was not so sure, and they had great difficulty in persuading the 'Old Man' to part with £500 to buy the first machine from Germany.

By now the Brown family had risen up the social ladder and had bought a house with 15 acres of land at Lockwood, about a mile and a half from Huddersfield. In one corner they built a small factory and Frank Brown went to live in Park Cottage at the other end of the field. By the early 1900s Huddersfield had become a rich town with several wealthy magnates who drove Rolls Royces, and ate and drank a great deal – David Brown was not one of them. In 1903 he died aged 60; he had been a hard man but a competent one.

Under David Brown's will Ernest inherited the pattern-making business, and the new gear business was shared equally between the three brothers, Ernest, Frank and Percy. Gradually Ernest severed his interest in the company and Frank and Percy became joint managing directors, until Percy died in 1931.

In 1902 the gear cutting machinery had been moved to the new 'Park Works', and the firm

Park Works in Huddersfield, 1902

became involved in the production of worm gears. However with electrification of the mills and with higher speed machines, involving the use of ball-bearings, design concepts took another leap forward. Parallel developments included the internal combustion engine, which led to the coming of motor buses, initially with chain drive, but now it was possible to install more effective worm gear axles. David Brown's were involved in all these innovations and took out a number of patents including the 'F.J.'

involute helicoidal thread on which the British Standard 721 of 1963 was based.

New work centred on the development of heat treated metals – life was work, there was little time for recreation. Although Frank Brown was a hard man in some ways, and the driving force behind the business, he was also a fair man – a story is told of him concerning five or six men aged about 70 who had been paid off; when he heard of it he offered them their jobs back, saying: "These are the people who have built up this business and there will be work for them as long as they can walk to it.' In 1912 the brothers turned the firm into a public company, to provide them with extra capital.

Some years earlier they had bought the manufacturing rights to two cars, the Dodson and the Valveless, the latter having a two stroke engine, but production had to cease at the outbreak of war in 1914.

The years of the First World War brought five-fold expansion in four years. Gear manufacturing was invaluable in vehicle production and soon Park Works was employing over 1000 men. Both wooden and concrete merchant ships were built to overcome a shortage of steel – David Brown's made the gearing for their propulsion as well as for destroyers, submarines and other warships. By the 1920s they were the largest worm gear manufacturer in the world. It was also at this time that the company developed the 'Roloid' geared pumps, which are still widely used today.

In 1921 David Brown, grandson of the founder, entered the company as an engineering apprentice. Born in Park Cottage on the site of the present works, it was said of him, when a baby, that he had 'oval arms and involute teeth'. Throughout his childhood his father 'soaked him in the business', opening the daily post and reading the letters to the young lad! As an apprentice he travelled six miles on a motorcycle to be at work for 7.30am; at home his father cross-examined him as to what he was learning.

When Armstrong-Whitworth amalgamated with Vickers, W S Roe left to join Brown's as works manager. Young David became his personal assistant with responsibility for the subsidiary Keighley Gear Company which he restored to profitibility before joining the main David Brown Board in 1929.

Following the death of Percy Brown, Frank became chairman and young David was appointed joint managing director along with W S Roe; after only eight weeks Roe died and David Brown became managing director, although not yet 30 years old. By the mid sixties, with David as chairman, the company employed about 20,000 people in the United Kingdom and overseas.

However it was the difficult thirties and they were overstaffed; cuts had to be made and he had to make them, but he developed a scheme of compensation based on years of service, something new in those days. He also appointed a sales manager, Allan Avison, who started as an

office boy and rose to become deputy managing director of the David Brown Corporation.

In 1930 the Brown family acquired P R Jackson Ltd of Salford, a steel foundry that also made machine moulded and machine cut gears. The founder, Peter Rothwell Jackson, had taken out patents in the 1800s relating to hydraulic presses, pumps and steam valves which had wide applications in the Lancashire textile industry – the company had a good history of scientific innovation. By the mid thirties Park Works was used to capacity and the iron and bronze foundries were moved to the former Cammell Laird Steel Works at Penistone where Brown's also began to produce high grade steels.

Another venture came in 1936 when a joint company was formed to build Ferguson tractors, but differences of opinion between David Brown and Harry Ferguson brought this to an end, although David Brown then set up his own tractor works at Meltham near Huddersfield. The new David Brown tractor, complete with a new engine, was launched at the Royal Agricultural Society's Show at Windsor in July 1939 and orders were taken for over 3000 tractors. The tractor was designed to carry mounted hydraulic implements, but also had a patented depth control wheel.

At one stage Meltham was the only factory left producing gears for the Merlin engine in the Spitfire fighter aircraft. By the end of the war Brown's, in their various plants, employed 6,000 staff.

Immediately after the war the company embarked on a number of major developments – building up agricultural tractor production, Aston-Martin and Lagonda cars (which David Brown personally purchased for about £80,000! – he led Aston Martin to win many

Assembling 11.6m diameter girth rings on copper ore grinding mills in Western Canada

Above, Sir David Brown; below, the elegant Aston Martin DB6

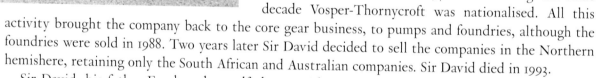

prestigious races, and ultimately the World Sports Car Championship in 1959), very high accuracy gear cutting machines from Muir Machine Tools, acquired in 1944, and a series of overseas ventures in gear manufacturing.

After his father's death, in 1941 David Brown increased his holding until he had complete control of the Equity Capital. Tractor production increased rapidly and following the acquisition of Hannon McGregor and Guest the Tractor Group turnover exceeded the Gear Group. The Gear Group achieved world market leadership in production of turbine gear cutting machines and measuring instruments. In 1949 they started gear manufacturing in South Africa and over the next 20 years entered other major countries. In 1960 David Brown Bingham was established to manufacture centrifugal pumps under licence and in 1964 David Brown acquired a controlling interest in the shipbuilders, Vosper, and later acquired John I Thornycroft; now they were capable of building destroyers! In 1968 David Brown received a knighthood for his services to industry and exports.

By 1948 the Gear Group had the capabilities to cut gears up to 40 feet in diameter; in 1984 with the installation of a Maag 1200 in South Africa the capacity increased to 14 metres diameter, and with greater accuracy! For financial reasons Sir David decided to sell off the tractor and car businesses in the 1970s and during the same decade Vosper-Thornycroft was nationalised. All this activity brought the company back to the core gear business, to pumps and foundries, although the foundries were sold in 1988. Two years later Sir David decided to sell the companies in the Northern hemishere, retaining only the South African and Australian companies. Sir David died in 1993.

Sir David, his father Frank and grandfather David served the family business between them for the whole 130 years. On receiving his knighthood in 1968 Sir David paid tribute to all the employees who had played their part in the development of the companies he controlled. The name lives on not only in the current company but as any classic car enthusiast knows, in the elegant D.B. Aston Martin produced by the company during the 25 years it was part of the David Brown Corporation. Following the management buy-in by the present chief executive Chris Brown and chairman Chris Cook, the David Brown Group plc, which now also includes the original David Brown southern hemisphere companies, has retained the tradition of quality and technical excellence and continues to be a world leader.

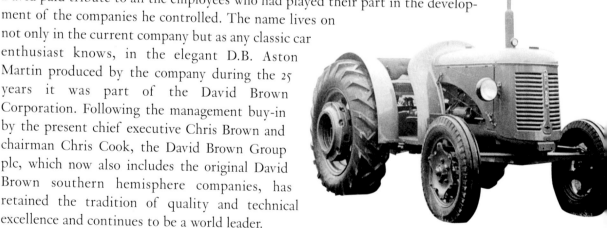

David Brown Cropmaster, 1948

Joseph (Joe) Corrigan came from Ireland in the late 1800s to live in Liverpool; he was a travelling fairman. When he was only fifteen he went to America. While still in his teens he went with a friend to Maryland in search of work and they were taken to the docks by two men who offered them a job. Once there they were separated and before he realised what was happening Joe was taken below and the ship's hatch was closed on top of him. Only when the ship was out to sea was he allowed on deck and told that the job was catching oysters, hopefully for their pearls – he had been 'shanghaied'! It was 96 days before they came near to land; to escape he swam three miles to the shore.

Joe eventually returned to England where he met Polly Morley; he was 26, she 18. He went to see Polly at her friend's house where he was asked to wait in a downstairs room for a few minutes. He was amazed when Polly and her friend re-appeared, for Polly was dressed in full bridal array. His shock was short lived, however, for Polly explained that it was not her dress! She was modelling the dress for her friend who believed it was bad luck to wear it herself before her wedding, but wanted to see how it looked. Nevertheless it must have stimulated Joe's interest for that night Joe proposed to Polly and the couple were married three weeks later! Their first home was a homemade caravan; simply a flat cart with a cotton top and cupboards made from a three compartment orange box, with chintz draped down the front; their light was a candle in a bottle.

Their first stands were a coconut shy and a striking machine, which they took from fair to fair. In winter Joe rented a flat cart at 6s a week, bought coal at 7s 6d a ton from a Leeds pit and sold the coal at 6d a hundredweight; it made them a comfortable living. Year by year the couple and their ever increasing family travelled from town to town, fair to fair. By 1901 they had six children and needed a new living wagon – it was delivered by rail in July to the Dewsbury Feast, a very fine one with a separate bedroom, something unique at the time, and much admired.

About this time Joe bought some steam swings and these brought him a lot of business.

Joe and Polly had ten children who survived, five sons and five daughters – Johnny, Joey, Edwin, Jimmy, Albert and Mary Jane, Bella, Sarah, Norah and Violet! Polly was 36 when Norah, the youngest child, was born; she had had fifteen pregnancies. As the children grew older each had a period of schooling for about three years. Johnny went on to become a Commonwealth heavyweight fighter and during

the 1929 National Strike the family ran boxing booths.

Back in the early 1900s business was generally good. In 1910 Joe bought a cinematograph show which measured 60 feet by 40 feet, the first film shown was 'The Last of the Mohicans' – films came on 1,000 foot reels which ran for 20 minutes. However they could only use it where there was no 'picture house' in the town and after three months the show must move on to another place. Later a Marenghi's organ was added and now the 'punters' could have an hour's show which comprised a travel film, Pathe Gazette, feature film and a cartoon – all for 2d!

Forty-eight hours after the coronation of King George V, in 1910, Corrigans had a film of the ceremony on view and a lot of people turned up to view it, but this was one of the last shows before the show was sold. Times were hard. Success only returned as they re-entered the fairs, but it was not until they started to take part in the larger West Riding fairs that they began to take reasonable amounts of money. In 1913 Joe bought back the old steam swings that seemed to have brought him so much luck in the early days; perhaps history would repeat itself!

One man who worked for the Corrigans was Billy Dolan, a big man who was the champion pea eater of the world – he had it tattooed on his chest.

Polly Corrigan, who fed the workers, always cooked Billy 5lbs of potatoes with meat and vegetables, and always a pudding to follow, usually made of suet, and whenever possible gave him a plate of tripe with vinegar! However with the outbreak of the First World War things had to change as several members of the family joined the armed forces.

After the war life returned to moving from fair to fair, often only putting up the stalls or rides for one or two days before taking them down again and moving on to the next town or village. By now the Corrigans had a sweet stall, coconut shies, a three abreast ride (where the horses go up and down – a carousel), a panham stall (sweets or brandysnap), dart stall, chairo-planes, steam swings and a housy-housy, to name but a few. In 1925 Joe Corrigan exchanged his barrel organ for a Gavioli 89 key paper organ which certainly attracted the crowds to his three abreast ride.

Two years later he was elected chairman of the Yorkshire Section of the Showmen's Guild and was invited to meet the Prince of Wales.

Above, Corrigan promoted this boxing event at Middlesbrough in 1929; left, the stall that sold everything

About this time Stanley Baldwin, the Prime Minister, attended a large Conservative rally near Beverley and came to visit Joe Corrigan at his showground, where he looked around his caravan and the large steam engine, Try Again. In 1930 Bella Corrigan married Jonas Holdsworth, a member of a well known Bradford family of showpeople, and today their son has the amusements at Filey.

That same winter Jimmy and Albert Corrigan noticed that the old skating rink in Dragon Road, Harrogate, was available and Joe leased it for three months, putting in dodgem cars, a ghost train and other attractions.

Polly died in 1939 bringing to an end over 40 years' association with the fairgrounds, and her matriarchal position in the family.

Albert and Jimmy bought the business from their father and during the war had 'Black Out Fairs', where everything was done behind sheeting. These stay at home fairs were done to keep morale high; one of them was held on the Stray at Harrogate, where they also had children's swings and roundabouts. Although petrol was on strict rationing the Corrigans were allowed supplies of petrol and diesel to allow them to move around and to run the generators which drove the large rides.

Through the early 1940s the family lived at Starbeck, near Harrogate, and did contracting for nearby farmers, using their heavy traction engines to do threshing at harvest time as part of the war effort.

When the war ended Albert and Jimmy bought an amusement park, The Jetty at Sandside at Scarborough, from a Mr Westall, which is now known as Lunar Park and is run by the Tubey family. Jimmy's nephew, Joey, branched out into another area of the entertainment business when in the 1960s he opened the Batley Variety Club which for over a decade presented artists from

Polly Corrigan shaking hands with the Prime Minister Stanley Baldwin. Joe Corrigan is at the foot of the steps

around the world to audiences of over 2000 people. Edwin Corrigan bought an amusement arcade at Filey, and Johnny Corrigan acquired one at Primrose Valley, Filey. Today Billy Holdsworth has the arcade at Coble Landing at Filey. while Jimmy Corrigan jnr has several entertainment enterprises in Scarborough.

Joe Corrigan died in 1960, but members of the wider Corrigan family are still involved in showmanship and amusement facilities from Northumberland to the coast of Kent.

JOHNSON
GROUP CLEANERS PLC

(CROCKATTS)

In 1814 Peter Campbell moved to Perth, setting up as a dyer, and by 1818 he had been admitted as a merchant burgess and was a respected citizen. Peter married a childless widow whose first husband, William Pullar, had died young. Later Peter took on 14 year old John Pullar, his wife's relative by her first marriage, as an apprentice. At the age of 21 John Pullar set up as a dyer in opposition to his former master, founding the well known firm of Pullars of Perth.

In 1847, Anne, the eldest child of Peter Campbell, married John Crockatt, a shipmaster of Tayport. They had three sons but by 1854 John Crockatt had died of cholera. One of his three sons, also John, became an apprentice dyer to Peter Campbell jnr in 1866 when he was 14 years old. In the first year he was paid four shillings for working a 60 hour week, with overtime as required; each year his wage rose by two shillings a week, reaching 14 shillings in the final year.

John Crockatt was a good apprentice but, at the end of his term knew he had to leave the

business as the Campbell family had sons to follow him. In April 1873 he joined a friend, Willie Watson, who was also a dyer, in Leeds but quickly moved on to Bradford, finding work with Josiah Leach in Brick Lane.

On a visit to Scotland, he learned from his mother the art of feather-curling and when he returned to Bradford he brought with him the requisite knives and bargained with his employer to do this specialised work.

At the end of the year he sought wider experience on the continent, but finding no work in Brussels he moved on to Paris, walking the 200 miles between the two cities in six days! By November 1874 he was back in England working as a dyer with Eastman of London in Oxford Street, but was so revolted by the dishonesty of the foreman dyer that he left after only six weeks

In the spring of 1875 he started his own business as a dyer and cleaner in Carlton Hill, Leeds. He rented a warehouse and yard, the landlord agreeing to supply 'twelve square yards of good stone flags'; these were for his dyehouse floor and John laid them himself and dug the drains. In those early days he had only two employees, his friend Willie Watson and an apprentice. John and his mother lived in nearby Blenheim Mount.

Above, John Crockatt, proprietor 1875-1920 and chairman 1920-27; right, the first motor van – a Model T Ford – purchased by Crockatt's in 1914

Having items cleaned or dyed was a luxury and his customers were mainly from the middle or upper classes. He soon realised that his premises were not ideally located for collected work and he opened a shop at 2a Commercial Street, in the heart of the city. By 1886 he had expanded into Harrogate and Wakefield and by 1903 he had eight premises in Leeds as well as sites at Harrogate, Wakefield, Hull, Morley and York. Initially articles to be cleaned were collected and returned by horse transport or sent by rail from more distant points. Later Crockatt boys on carrier bicycles became a common sight collecting and delivering to customers' homes.

John Crockatt had four sons, two became dyers and two became doctors. Arthur J Crockatt, the eldest son, described for us the Works as they were in his father's day. It was a three storey building with a packing room, dyehouse, boiler room, a room containing a damask press, a benzine room, a carpet-beating room, two rooms in which curtains were processed, an ironing room, and stables. One piece of equipment consisted of a cylinder about eight feet long and seven feet in diameter. Into this was placed sawdust which had been well damped with cleaning spirit. The carpets were revolved in the drum for half an hour and then taken out, beaten again and dried. It wasn't a satisfactory method. The feather curling skills now became important as they cleaned and curled the fashionable ostrich feathers worn in ladies' hats and feather boas.

John Crockatt kept his own books and also acted as wages clerk, paying each man his wages from piles of coins on his desk. John knew each employee by name – no doubt he had set them on. Many of his early workers referred to him as 'Father', for he was white-haired at an early age, but he also belonged to that group of employers who were patriarchal, being influenced by their non-conformist traditional Christianity and their radical politics. In 1910 the works moved to

The hosiery was mended by hand in the 1920s

a new site in Stoney Rock Lane, Burmantofts, beyond which were acres of fields of rhubarb. In 1914 the firm bought some Model T Fords, and horses were phased out.

After the end of the First World War John's two sons, Arthur and Douglas, rejoined the firm. Arthur was a scientist and technologist and Douglas supplied financial and commercial drive to the operation. In 1920 the works were expanded from 18,000 square feet to 30,000 square feet and the number of shops had grown from the 14 of a decade earlier to 30. John Crockatt died in 1927 aged 75. He had laid the foundations which enabled the business to spread into north Lincolnshire and later into Manchester.

In 1928 Crockatts had declined to join the Johnson Group of Dyers and Cleaners and it was not until 1935 that the merger was agreed. The decision was influenced by the belief that war

was coming, with the possibility of bombing, and the company would be safer as part of a group of five firms. In acknowledgement of Douglas Crockatt's management abilities he was immediately invited to join the Johnson Board. In 1938 the group acquired the Pullar-Eastman combine and Douglas Crockatt joined that Board, renewing the family link with Perth and the Pullar and former Campbell businesses. Later Arthur Crockatt became a director of the Eastman enterprises, renewing the link formed by John Crockatt's employment in 1874.

As the Crockatts had anticipated, the Johnson plant in Liverpool was damaged by a bomb during the Second World War. This resulted in major workload replanning and all Johnson's Yorkshire work had to be done at the Stoney Rock Lane site.

At the end of the war Crockatts had 79 shops and Douglas Crockatt observed: "A business is much more than a pile of assets – bricks and mortar, machinery and dry figures in ledgers. A business consists essentially of PEOPLE working together for a common end – and we forget it at our peril." He became group chairman from 1952-1966.

A further generation of the Crockatt family had now entered the business, destined for top positions. But commercial times were changing.

The changing face of cleaning... top, Crockatt's transport of the 1950s; above, the Bramley branch when it opened in 1975; below, the recently introduced drive-in service

Versatile mini-dry cleaning plants became available which could be bought on hire-purchase and which operated in the shops. As the number of shops increased to 125, the importance of the Stoney Rock Lane works decreased.

The last twenty years have seen further changes. The Johnson Group now operates in the United States, and is divided in the UK into Johnson Cleaners UK Ltd and Apparelmaster UK Ltd. Much of the work is servicing the food industry with clean garments, as well as offering a workwear garment rental service to other firms. Other new developments are concessions in supermarket chains and the growth of drive-in and out-of-town sites.

Dacre, Son & Hartley

John Dacre, was born in the small village of Bramhope, three miles from the busy market town of Otley, in 1790. In 1813 he married Hannah Saxton, the daughter of the village carpenter, and although he was then described as cordwainer, by 1820 he was more fully described as 'shoemaker and collector of taxes'.

A tax collector was an important person. It was a time of great poverty and often agricultural labourers and workers in textile mills had little alternative but to pay their dues in 'kind'. This meant that the tax collector had to be able to value items such as pigs, eggs or other stock-in-trade. It was a good apprenticeship for the business which was to become John Dacre's life.

In 1820 the office equipment consisted of a quill pen, paper and a candle, and transport would be by pack horse or stage coach. The firm began in John Dacre's front room in his home in Bramhope, and it was not until 1847 that he moved his business into Otley, to premises in busy Bondgate. He was described as 'Auctioneer and Appraiser, Northern Counties Association'. Otley was an important centre, both as a manufacturing base and also as a market town serving the local and more widely dispersed agricultural community; an ideal location for John Dacre's business.

From 1850 the business was conducted in a house and shop in Northgate, or Bridge Street as

Company founder John Dacre

it is known today. John Dacre died in 1860 and was succeeded by his son, also named John who was born in 1820, the year the firm was founded. Father and son not only laid the firm foundation of the business but also developed it over a wide area, bearing in mind that the only transport available to them in the early days was the horse. The records of those early days are interesting, dealing with the furniture, linen and plate they auctioned, and the valuation and sale of personal clothing. They became respected in the agricultural community for their abilities in the valuation of farmland, growing crops and livestock.

One of their most interesting commissions was to conduct a valuation of the stables at Goldsborough Hall in 1859, for the Dowager Duchess of Harewood. The total value amounted to £579 7s 6d, and included four Hansoms, a Toby carriage, a dog cart, a bath chair, a state harness, and four sets of horse harness. Their work was now taking them to Newark and Wakefield as well as the nearby Dales.

In 1845 young John Dacre married Rachael, the daughter of Samuel Bentley, 'clerk and flour dealer, Bramhope', and when John Dacre jnr died in 1869 their eldest son Charles Bentley Dacre succeeded to the business, although only 21 years old. In spite of his youth he was energetic, possessed a shrewd business mind and was a good auctioneer and valuer. His particular interest was in agricultural and livestock valuations which was central to their work in such a rural area. He started an auction mart, complete with sale ring and pens, on the west side of Station Road, which became known as the Otley Livestock Auction Mart. When it opened in 1875 it answered a long felt need in Wharfedale by offering cattle, sheep and pigs for unreserved sale. It was subsequently taken over by J Lister and became the Wharfedale Farmer's Auction Mart.

In 1881 Dacre & Son moved to Station Road in Otley, on the opposite side of the road to the present offices, and in 1886 acquired a block of shops on the corner of Station Road and Burras Lane, and converted them into offices.

Many are the tales told of the exploits of the founder and his son as they went about their business among a wide range of mainly Yorkshire people. One involves Sir Titus Salt of Saltaire. He had a dispute with a tenant farmer and Dacre & Son were called in to arbitrate. When they had completed their arbitration Sir Titus was informed that the valuation was ready and would be issued on payment of the three guineas fee. Sir Titus replied

that it was not his custom to pay for anything until he had seen it, and if the award was sent to him then he would pay the fee. Dacre & Son was a well established firm and not easily daunted; awards were customarily not issued until fees had been paid, and Sir Titus was not to be an exception to the rule! Correspondence regarding the matter went on for two years, but still Dacre & Son did not receive their three guineas, but neither did Sir Titus Salt receive his award!

John Dacre jnr also had two younger sons; Henry became a solicitor in the town and John William became an auctioneer and valuer, at first on his own account, but later in 1889 with Dacre & Son, and on the death of Charles Bentley Dacre in 1899, he became its head.

John William Dacre died in 1926 and the firm was purchased by Alleyne W S Berry of Hull who was the sole proprietor until 1932 when the business was sold to Douglas H Smallwood. The character of the practice now began to change from its estate agency and agricultural background to include the sale and letting of industrial and commercial properties. Other new areas of expertise concerned rating appeals and the valuation of industrial plant and machinery for insurance purposes.

Thomas Hartley had established a business in Ilkley in 1906 which included the sale of household furnishings, auctioneering and undertaking. When he died in 1924 his son Douglas took over the auctioneering but after a short period he moved to work with another auctioneer in Scarborough. However in 1927 he returned to Ilkley to his former role.

The premises were now in Tower Buildings, at the bottom of Cowpasture Road, but in 1928 the firm moved to 11 The Grove, Ilkley and opened an additional office at 10 Boroughgate in Otley in 1929. When Douglas Hartley later opened an office in Station Road, Otley he was in competition with Dacre & Son, for their offices were almost opposite each other.

In 1936 the two practices amalgamated under the title of Dacre, Son & Hartley, a title that has remained to the present day. When Douglas Smallwood had taken over Dacre & Son in 1932 he was only 21 years old but he already had his own practice in the town. Later he became prominent in the town, and in his profession, and became Chairman of the Otley Town Council. As the firm expanded Douglas' younger brother, John North Smallwood, became a partner and opened an office in Skipton. John soon discovered that he was getting a lot of work in the Keighley area and it was agreed that he open an office at 24 Devonshire Street, Keighley.

During the second world war Douglas Hartley was engaged with war damage claims, for the government, in Hull whilst Douglas Smallwood operated both the Ilkley and Otley offices, with John Smallwood at Keighley. After the war the partners purchased the present Ilkley premises at the bottom of Wells Road, along with a saleroom on Little Lane. In Keighley the Temperance Hall was rented to be used as a saleroom for furniture, antiques, etc. The Skipton office, which originally was at 1 Otley Street, was in rooms over Clitheroe's grocer's shop with access through a passageway. During the war years this office was closed down but in 1967 more appropriate offices in Sheep Street were opened.

In 1987 Dacre, Son & Hartley became a limited company but in 1989 was taken over by Abbey National as part of their Cornerstone group of estate agents. However the partners had insisted that the name Dacre, Son & Hartley be retained and this was unique throughout the group.

Following a management buy back in October

Otley livestock mart offered a new facility when it opened in 1875

1995 Dacre, Son & Hartley again returned to local ownership with Jim Horsley as Chairman and Martin Thompson as Managing Director.

Today Dacre, Son & Hartley operate from 19 offices across the county, Ilkley being the company's registered office, although their business activities stretch the length of the country. The company is involved in land development and planning issues, management of both residential and commercial properties, and the sale and acquisition of licenced premises; the valuation of industrial plant and machinery has already taken them to Belgium and Africa!

The company also manages extensive areas of grouse moor and agricultural estates as well as acting for many well-known national companies. Recent expansion includes new commercial offices in Leeds and Bradford.

DALESMAN

Harry J Scott was born in Plymouth in 1903 but when he was very young his parents moved north, eventually settling in Hyde Park, Leeds. Harry was brought up in a family with a strong Quaker background. He wanted to be an architect but the cost of training was such that it was decided he should become an accountant. Eventually he left accountancy and became a journalist with the Yorkshire Evening News, and then with the Yorkshire Post.

The young journalist married the love of his life, Dorothy, and they had two children, Martin and Margaret. Harry and Dorothy loved the Dales and took the family away from the city for a month or so each year into the Washburn Valley to Folly Hall where they rented part of a farm. They never had a car and Harry walked into Otley then caught the bus into Leeds to the office. He was determined to break loose

from Leeds. He began jotting down details of life in the Dales, fascinating stories of the folk who lived there and the customs they still kept. Perhaps it was this which encouraged him to seek a job with Robertson Scott, the founder of the Countryman, in Burford, Oxfordshire.

It was fortunate, almost providential, that he did not get the job for soon afterwards it became clear to him that he really wanted to start his own magazine, a magazine created in the Dales about the Dales, and for the Dales folk; but could it work, would he be able to make it pay? Then Harry saw an advertisement in the Yorkshire Post for a 'little house' to rent in Clapham. He wasted no time in taking the family to see the place and they fell in love with it. Standing in the shadow of Ingleborough, it cost 10 shillings a week.

Harry reckoned that if he could earn £3 a week with the Yorkshire Post they would be able to pay their way. Over the next few years he travelled daily, by train, to Leeds to continue working at the Yorkshire Post. His fellow journalists had seen the shoe box filled with 'material' for the project; perhaps they were sceptical but the vision was soon put to the test. With financial help from Linton Andrews, editor of the Leeds Mercury who later became editor of the Yorkshire Post, and six other friends, all of whom put up loans of £50, a start was made! Even so there was plenty of comment such as Yorkshire folk were 'tight wi' ther' brass', they were too hard-headed to be interested in a magazine about themselves and 'tha'll loss more ner tha addles'.

In Clapham, in the house they now call 'Fellside', Harry took over the front parlour where the magazine's 28 pages of material and outside cover were hand-set, before being

Harry J Scott

printed by Lamberts in Settle. 3,000 copies were printed, for which he paid £25. This first The Yorkshire Dalesman cost 3d, or 3 shillings 6 pence per annum post free! It was black and white, except for the cover which was printed on buff tinted heavy paper and it included a letter from 'Mr J B Priestley' wishing The Yorkshire Dalesman success. Among other contributors were Ella Pontefract, Marmaduke and Norman Thornber, a local corn merchant. Even in that first issue there was 'A Yorkshire Dalesman's Diary', a regular feature to the present day, as well as 'Readers' Club', still a popular feature.

Marie Hartley, Ella Pontefract, Joan Ingleby and Kit Calvert were most encouraging and a few people had been persuaded to advertise in it, among them Awmacks of Leeds, Settle & District Publicity Association and some hotels and boarding houses. Norman Thornber helped with the 'distribution' – taking bundles of copies, on sale or return, to nearby newsagents who were not enthusiastic about the idea. During those first months circulation increased, but hopes took a buffeting when war was declared.

The number of copies had to be reduced to a maximum of 4,000, with fewer pages, and on poorer quality paper. As numbers had to decrease, costs rose and it almost looked as if the little venture might have to close. However there was such a demand from those serving 'King & Country' around the world that Harry and Dorothy knew they had to keep faith with their readers.

By now it was a 'family' business, keeping the accounts, answering correspondence or tying parcels and addressing envelopes; even young Martin and Margaret took letters and parcels to the village post office in the garden wheelbarrow! To help the family budget Harry got an editorial job with the Craven Herald & Pioneer in Skipton.

In 1943 a young W R (Bill) Mitchell started work at the Craven Herald & Pioneer and in 1948 joined the staff of The Dalesman, beginning a long association with the magazine, later becoming editor.

By 1955 circulation reached over 25,000, and a sister magazine, Cumbria, covering the Lake District was acquired. It was time to increase the 'office', and space was taken in the former coach house and estate workshops in Clapham.

OLD AMOS

"If at first thou doesn't succeed – ask thissen why!"

Old Amos, a regular in the magazine since the 1940s, was created by Rowland Lindup and is continued today by his son Pete; below, an early advertisement for a popular Dalesman book

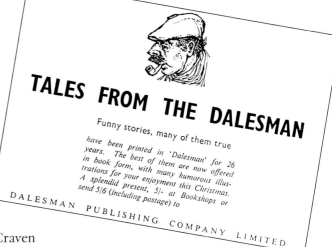

TALES FROM THE DALESMAN

Funny stories, many of them true have been printed in 'Dalesman' for 26 years. The best of them are now offered in book form, with many humorous illustrations for your enjoyment this Christmas. A splendid present, 5/- at Bookshops or send 5/6 (including postage) to

DALESMAN PUBLISHING COMPANY LIMITED

When Dennis Bullock, who later became managing director, joined the company in 1961, his first task was to open the morning's mail. In those days, he discovered, this took place amidst the toast and marmalade, remnants of breakfast! Still the family 'suffered' parcels of magazines freshly arrived from the printers, often covered by a table-cloth and supporting a vase of flowers.

Gradually the circulation rose, settling at an impressive 65,000, making it the premier regional magazine. When Harry Scott took semi-retirement Bill Mitchell assumed editorial control and the future of the Dalesman was ensured by transferring ownership to its four longest-serving employees. Sadly in January 1978 Harry J Scott died and the Dales lost a humble man who had seen his vision develop into an institution. His ashes were scattered in his beloved Clapham.

Left, Bill Mitchell, who joined Dalesman in 1948 and retired in 1988; below, magazine covers from 1952, the 50th anniversary edition in 1989, and 1997

The current editor, Terry Fletcher, is only the magazine's fourth in almost sixty years. Like Harry Scott, he comes from a background in Yorkshire newspaper journalism and he is already successfully building on the heritage of the magazine's founder.

Dalesman Publishing Company has also been notable for its many books. In the early days Alfred Wainwright had offered Harry Scott the opportunity to publish the first of his Lakeland books, which sadly Harry had to decline.

More recently Dennis Bullock and his co-directors were fortunate to find successors able to steer Dalesman quietly through the technological revolution, which has so affected the whole of publishing, whilst at the same time safeguarding Dalesman's long traditions.

J B Priestley wrote in 1965 in Life International: "Harry Scott is one of those rare and fortunate newspapermen who have made a familiar dream come true. He founded and edited his own monthly magazine." How well Harry Scott lived up to his own ambitions is witnessed by the fulfilment of "the very practical aims" he stated for Dalesman in its first issue, "of interesting all who love the Dales; of providing a link between the Dales, its places, people and activities and those who cannot enjoy its deep satisfaction at first hand; and by no means of least importance of furthering the well being of the Dales country and its people."

Double Two®
Est. 1940

THE NEW SHIRT BLOUSE WITH SPARE COLLAR..... TO WEAR OPEN OR BUTTONED UP

INSTRUCTIONS

Engl. Patent No. 503354

Buy one have two

1 When the first collar begins to show signs of wear—pull the loop underneath the collar and the worn collar will drop off neatly and easily.

2 Now take the spare collar which must first be washed and ironed. It is identical with the old one, and is going to fit you just as perfectly—thanks to a special groove which you'll find in the neckband of the shirt.

3 Fit the collar into the groove and sew it in. Without spending a penny the shirt is ready to wear—like new. Double-Two Shirts are made with single or double cuffs. In the case of double cuffs spare cuffs are supplied, changeable on the same easy principle.

In 1869 William Sugden married Ann Mortimer and started business as a tailor in Railway Street, Cleckheaton. As the years passed William also acquired a draper's shop, where their children, four boys and a girl, joined him when they left school.

In 1896 the two eldest sons, Allan and Bernard, started to make shirts, sharing a sewing machine, in the room behind the shop. During the first three years they made no profits but in 1899 they broke even, started to expand, and moved to Water Lane Mills in Cleckheaton. They opened a factory in Barnsley in 1904 and started manufacturing in Wakefield in 1911, moving to bigger premises in Wakefield in 1924. By now their main trade was in shirts, pyjamas and overalls for working men, under the name 'Water Lane Brand'. They sold their garments to small independent retailers, and to pawnbrokers who abounded in every town at that time.

During the 1920s the company acquired two weaving mills where they wove all the cotton drill for the garments which were made up in their own factories. Between 1939 and 1945 the company made over five million shirts and worksuits for the armed forces.

After the war major changes took place, particularly the large increases in imports, which meant that Sugdens also had to change. In the early 1960s polyester/cotton fabrics were introduced and it was soon realised that not only did they look smarter but were easier to care for, and cotton was gradually phased out. To meet the demand for easy-care shirts, the 'Topflight' shirt was developed, which would withstand the rigours of rental laundries and still look smart.

By 1968 they had disposed of their weaving mills, and in that year they sold their shareholding to 'Double Two', a shirt manufacturing company started in 1940 by Isaak Donner and Frank Myers, which traded as the Wakefield Shirt Company.

Until 1946 most of that company's production was ladies' tailored blouses, as plentiful supplies of rayon were available, but cotton for men's shirts was in short supply. Many women, working in factories during the war years, needed shirt-like blouses and the company produced them. In 1946, with men returning to 'civvy street', there was a demand for the soft collar-attached shirts which they had seen the American soldiers wearing.

Isaak Donner, founder along with Frank Myers of the Wakefield Shirt Company

However, British housewives were concerned that this new American style shirt would have to be thrown away when the collar wore out. The Donners overcame this problem with the invention of a shirt with a soft attached collar which was detachable by pulling a tape at the back of the neckband; a spare collar was supplied with each shirt. Initially, until stopped by the Board of Trade, who were concerned at the excessive use of 'strategic' material (cotton), Double Two also supplied a spare pair of cuffs for each shirt – 2 collars and 2 pairs of cuffs, hence the name 'Double Two'!

In the early 1950s Double Two launched the 'Terylene' shirt, the first man-made fibre shirt to be made in a knitted material, a non-iron shirt which was comfortable to wear. This brought the company great prosperity and at that time they employed 500 work people, produced nearly 800,000 shirts a year, and built a larger modern factory.

In the late '50s and through the '60s Double Two continued to be innovative with new fibre mixes for their material. In 1965 they introduced 'White Light', Europe's first permanent press shirt in 100% cotton – helped by a massive advertising campaign it achieved brand leadership in six months! As cheap imported shirts started to impact on the British market Double Two launched 'That Shirt by Double Two', shirts aimed at the fashion market where design and quick delivery of the latest styles were more important than price.

In 1968 Isaak Donner and his son Richard were joined by David and John Sugden and together they sought to move the combined companies even further forward as they met their wider markets.

Later L J & M Refson, a Sunderland based ladies' uniform and careerwear company, joined the group.

Today The Wakefield Shirt Company employs over 750 people in five factories. The company produces over three million garments a year and exports to about 70 countries world-wide. Today half the company's business is supplying corporate clothing and careerwear to the police, fire and ambulance services, and companies like the AA; they also supply own brand clothing to BHS, Next and the Burton Group.

ALBERT FARNELL DRIVING
THE ORANGE BOX WHICH
HE DESIGNED AND BUILT

100 YEARS'
SALES & SERVICE

Albert Farnell was born in Bradford in 1863. As a young man he became a keen and successful long distance cyclist, winning the 100 Guineas Yorkshire Trophy, and in 1887 covering 210 miles in a 24 hour cycle ride for the North Road Cycling Club. He married Emily Brown Watmough and it is believed she helped him with money he needed to start a business, selling cycles at Cross Lane, in the Great Horton area of the city.

He moved the business to 38 Manningham Lane where, in addition to advertising himself as 'The Cycle Engineer', he 'has now fitted up a department for the Repairing of all kinds of Domestic Machinery: Sewing Machines, Wringing Machines, Coffee Mills, &C.' Wringing Machine Rollers put in for 8/-, 10/-, 12/-, 15/- and 18/- per pair.'

In those early days he designed and made bicycles which he then sold, these being particularly popular among the middle class. In the early 1890s he designed his own cross-braced frame motor cycle with an air cooled engine, and started limited production. However, he saw a great future for the horseless carriage and his first automobile was called the 'Orange Box', because it had no body! It had a $\frac{1}{4}$hp air-cooled motor, which was belt driven, and had independent springs on the front wheels. The chassis was tubular, and later he fitted the vehicle with a patent four-speed non-crash gearbox. It was capable of 16mph using petrol, at that time called benzoline, which cost 8d a gallon and was purchased from the local plumbers.

The Great Horseless Carriage Co, of Coventry, in 1895 changed its name to The Daimler Motor Co Ltd and Albert Farnell was a member of the British Motor Syndicate which bought the Daimler patent and he became their sole agent in the North of England. The first Daimler he sold had wooden brakes which were operated by ropes; it ran at four speeds – five, ten, fifteen and twenty miles per hour.

When the Rover Cycle

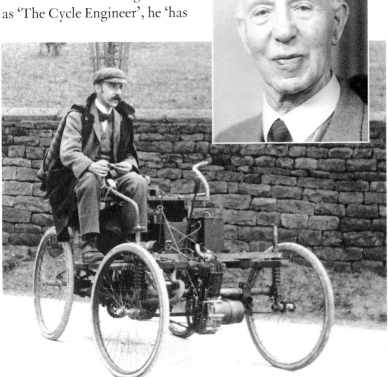

Left, the first motor car built by Albert Farnell (inset) in 1897

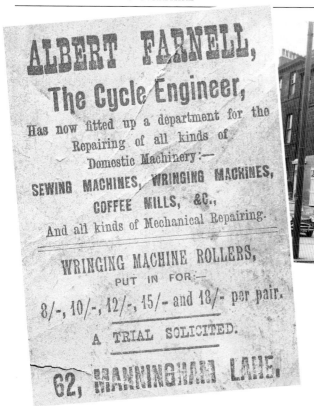

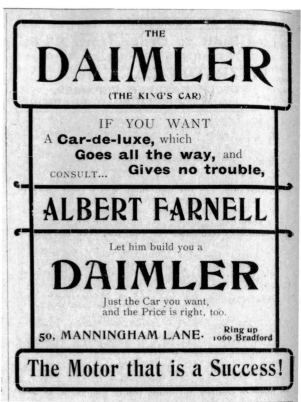

Left, a Farnell advertisement for from the 1890s; above, the Manningham Lane premises in the 1950s; below, Farnell's 1904 advertisement for Daimler as it appeared in The Jackdaw magazine

Company was formed he was also one of its first agents, later helping Edmund W Lewis to design his first Rover car, an 8hp single cylinder vehicle; at that time Lewis was in Bradford working on a steam bus for Italy. When Albert Farnell also took on Rover's agency for automobiles his territory included Skipton, Settle, Bowes and parts of the North Riding.

In 1904 he was advertising the De Dion – 'The De Dion has more power, will run more days in the year, is more simple to drive, more comfortable to ride in, than any other car at a similar price. My records show it.'

Albert was the owner of Bradford's first car registration numbers, AK 1 and AK 2 – they are still held by the company.

In those early years of the 20th century there was competitive racing in the Isle of Man between motor vehicles, using a similar course to the one used today for motorcycles, and here

Below, in the 1960s Farnell was selling Heralds as this Dalesman advertisement shows; right, launched in 1997, the Land Rover Freelander

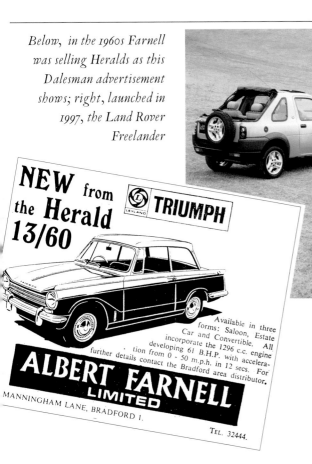

NEW from the Herald 13/60

TRIUMPH LEYLAND

Available in three forms: Saloon, Estate Car and Convertible. All incorporate the 1296 c.c. engine developing 61 B.H.P. with accelera-tion from 0 - 50 m.p.h. in 12 secs. For further details contact the Bradford area distributor.

ALBERT FARNELL LIMITED

MANNINGHAM LANE, BRADFORD 1.

TEL. 32444.

Albert raced his 70hp Daimlers at speeds exceeding 70mph. These cars had no windscreens to give protection from the dust which flew up from the unsurfaced roads. In 1912 the company was appointed Standard distributors.

Albert cared little for the new-fangled regulations which came in following the passing of the Road Traffic Act of 1930 and 1933, regulations such as having to obey speed limits!

Albert had a son Maurice from his first marriage and three children from his second marriage – Ina, Gladys and Lewis. In the 1920s he took his family on alpine holidays, a rare occurrence at that time.

In 1943 a severe fire destroyed the premises, the fire having started in a billiard room over Albert's business. A new building was erected on the same site, but set back from the road, to provide forecourt parking for customers. Albert had not been insured and therefore it was decided that the firm should become a private limited company. The Land Rover was introduced in 1948 and Farnell's became agents for it in 1949.

Albert died in 1951 – he had been in charge for 69 years – and was succeeded by Lewis, his nephew, as managing director. He had had a full life. When Lewis Farnell died in 1976 his son Arthur took control of the company and today the business is run by brothers Ian and David Farnell, sons of Arthur and great-grand-nephews of the founder.

In 1984 Farnell's moved from Bradford to Guiseley, where the company has its car showrooms, and in 1991 opened additional premises at Frizinghall, less than a mile from the Manningham Lane site, where they sell Land Rovers and Range Rovers; they started selling Land Rovers in 1948. Farnell's have been selling Rover products for over 100 years, something no other dealer in Yorkshire can claim, and are founder members of the Motor Agents Association, and hold membership number 2 of the Retail Motor Industries Federation!

An old booklet dating from about 1913 states that: "In a small unpretentious shop in the plain, whitewashed building which once adjoined the old-time hostelry, famous as the Crescent Inn, presided a homely old lady named Farrah. This was seventy years ago, and two years after Queen Victoria's accession to the Throne. Compared with other shops of that date this little store had few attractions. One, however, it possessed, destined to carry the name of Farrah to the end of time – Toffee! Even in those early days carriages blocked the narrow way of Crescent Road out of all harmony with the meagre display in those bulging small-paned windows. At the door mingled the idle patrician with the bustling housewife, the dishevelled maid, the awkward schoolboy, all intent on the same errand – Farrah's Toffee. Such Toffee! None could understand or withstand the magic of its seductive charm."

The "old lady Farrah" must have been Ann Farrah, widow of farmer Joseph Farrah. She died in 1843, age 74. However the booklet of 1913 suggests that the original coffee shop was owned by a Robert Swan. He was certainly in the area in 1841 when he was described as a man of 'independent means', so presumably he was quite wealthy. By the 1850s he was listed as Robert Hudson Swan, a grocer, tea-dealer and coffee-roaster at Victoria Tea-House, Promenade Square in Low Harrogate. He also leased the Pump Room from the Harrogate Improvement Commissioners around this period.

In those early days the toffee would have been cooked in open pans and stirred by hand, with the tempting smell wafting over the nearby area. No doubt the popularity of the toffee increased as people realised that sucking it helped to take away the unpleasant taste of some of the spa waters.

After Ann Farrah's death, her son Joseph took over as "Shopkeeper and Dealer in Groceries and Sundries" according to an 1848 directory. Later directories describe him as "Bread Baker", "Provisions-Dealer", and by 1873 "Toffee Maker" at 2 Crescent Place. In 1873 William Jefferson, of West Park, was advertising that he sold 'Harrogate Toffee', and later in 1879 Wm J Binns had a similar advertisement. Presumably John Farrah's register-

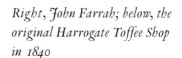

Right, John Farrah; below, the original Harrogate Toffee Shop in 1840

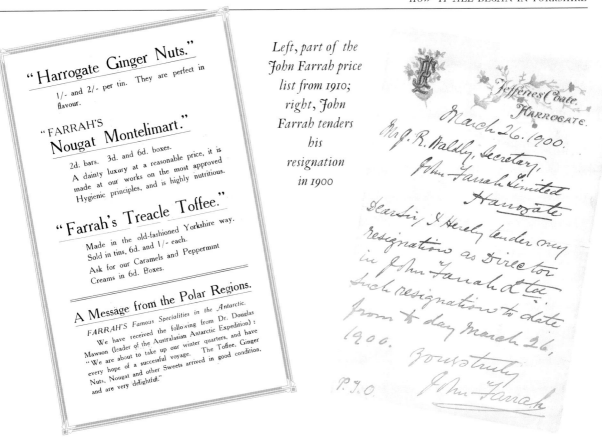

Left, part of the
John Farrah price
list from 1910;
right, John
Farrah tenders
his
resignation
in 1900

ing of 'Farrah's Harrogate Toffee' in 1887 was to establish his as the original.

Joseph married Esther Varley, and their only surviving son John was born in 1849. It is John's signature that appears on the famous blue and silver tins. Joseph had died by March 1879, the month in which John married Georgiana Livingstone Forbes of Low Harrogate. (According to one of his obituaries he actually married three times.)

John carried on the business after his father's death and appears to have expanded it. However it wasn't until 22 April 1887 that he registered the trade mark 'John Farrah'. John Farrah Ltd was formed on 16 February 1897, the directors being John Farrah, Fred Farrah Ridsdale, and Fred Hunter.

It would seem that John Farrah lost his interest

in the business, for in a letter to the company secretary, dated 26 March 1900, he tendered his resignation as a director in John Farrah Ltd. and offered his shares to the other directors. In 1901 the directors purchased 7 Royal Parade, described as a shop and house, from Mrs Stead for £3750.

John Farrah died in 1907, aged 58. In his obituaries he is described as a noted naturalist, and although it mentions that he had been 'formerly one of the leading tradesmen of the town as a grocer, baker and provision merchant, latterly in Crescent Road, and he was the founder of Messrs. John Farrah Ltd prior to his retiring from business', no mention is made of the Harrogate Toffee. Since his retirement he had bought West Syke Farm and White Wall Farm at Felliscliffe, on the outskirts of Harrogate, and there had pursued his interest in natural history.

The Crescent Road premises at the turn of the century; below, an advertisement from Punch magazine, 1949

John Farrah's obituaries described him as being "a man of many good qualities", and "exceptionally straightforward". He liked to be addressed as plain "John Farrah", disliking titles like "Mr" and "Esquire". He had one of the best scientific libraries in the district and was particularly interested in botany, geology and meteorology; for many years he was president of the Yorkshire Naturalists Union. He had three children, John William, (his eldest son who died only a few weeks before him), Joseph Sumpster and Constance Annie. In the early days of this century such well known London stores as Harrods, and Fortnum & Mason, were supplied direct with the now famous Farrah's Harrogate Toffee. Between the two world wars Farrah's exhibited their toffee at many exhibitions both in the United Kingdom and on the continent and were awarded medals for the quality of their product and its presentation.

During the Second World War, supplies of the ingredients for the Toffee, such as butter, sugar, treacle, glucose, etc. were in limited supply and packing materials hard to come by, but the firm continued to make small quantities. Female staff continued the work while the men were away.

Cyril Waddington had worked in the office of a carpet fibre manufacturer in Dewsbury but his father, a police sergeant, was moved to Harrogate and Cyril joined John Farrah Ltd in 1920. In 1954 Cyril's son Michael joined the firm and the following year the company moved its production department from behind the shop to new premises about two miles away. Although new machinery was installed, the toffee was still cooked in open copper pans and stirred by hand with oak paddles. The precise recipe, however, is still a secret, locked securely away in the vaults of a bank, but it is said that Farrah's Harrogate Toffee contains an especially high proportion of butter, one of the factors that gives it its special taste. Michael Waddington eventually became managing director, a position he held until he decided to close the firm in January 1997. It seemed that an important part of the life of Harrogate, and beyond, had finished. No more would people enjoy that renowned Farrah's Harrogate Toffee. However in March 1997 it was announced that Gary Marston, a Harrogate confectioner, had bought the company and saved the famous Harrogate Toffee.

Antonio Fattorini was born in the Italian village of Bellagio, on the shores of Lake Como, in 1797. It was the time of the French Revolution, the rise of Napoleon, and with his native Lombardy under threat from the Gallic forces Antonio, at the age of eighteen, decided to join the action in Belgium.

One day he was up a tree gathering mulberry leaves for silkworms when a party of young men passed through his village. He joined them, making his way by mule track through the St. Gotthard Pass to Switzerland and Germany before finally reaching Brussels. However, by the time they reached the war zone the Battle of Waterloo was already over and Napoleon had been driven from the world stage.

Young Antonio and a group of his new colleagues now headed for England. He arrived in Dewsbury – we do not know why he chose this town – which then had a population of about 8,000 people. The town had a reputation as a centre for pedlars and itinerant salesmen and within a few years Antonio had obtained a licence to sell goods in this way. He loaded his donkey with jewellery and set off to make his way in the world. Little did he know that those hard days and harsh winters would lead to better days and a rich business in years to come.

Antonio married a Leeds girl, Maria Broni, in 1824 in Leeds, and set up a stall in the new central market which had opened in 1827, Leeds being one of the first market towns which were gradually to replace the country fairs. On his stall he sold fancy goods, pots and pans, kneepads and similar items.

By 1830 the couple had three sons and the time had come for Antonio to make his next decisive move. He gave up his stall and moved his business into one of the tiny lock-up shops

Antonio Fattorini who started trading in Dewsbury in the early part of the 19th century; below, an extract from the Harrogate Advertiser of 1837

ORIENTAL LOUNGE,
High-Harrogate.

A. FATTORINI,

RESPECTFULLY announces to the Visitors and Inhabitants of Harrogate, that he has on hand a large
STOCK OF JEWELLERY,
Sheffield Plated Goods and Berlin Silver, which he is enabled to offer at extremely low prices.
Also Ladies, and Gentlemen's Dressing Cases, Writing Desk, Work Boxes, Umbrellas, Parasols, and a variety of other articles.
Cut Glass Decanters,
Tumblers, and a variety of Table Lamps, &c. &c.
August 10th, 1837.

FATTORINI AND SONS,
Watch & Chronometer Manufacturers,
GOLD & SILVERSMITHS, JEWELLERS, &c.,
2, Royal Parade, Harrogate,

Beg to announce that their Harrogate Establishment is now replete
with every variety of Stock kept by them. The following is an outline—

GOLD ENGLISH LEVERS,

From £9 to £100,

Gold Geneva Levers, Horizontals, ¾ Plates, &c.,

LADIES' GOLD WATCH,

18 Carat Cases, Warranted, for £3 3s.

ENGLISH PATENT LEVER, Capped, Jewelled, Maintaining Power,
and strong Silver Cases, £4.

SILVER PATENT LEVER,

Our own Manufacture, warranted for five years, £5.

These Watches are the best that can be produced at any price; hundreds of them are in use in the surrounding district, also along the
principal railway lines in the country, and their value and accurate
performance is fully testified by the ever increasing demand for them by
friends of the parties who have them in use.

Clocks of every description, going from 30 hours to one month. Our
Celebrated GUINEA STRIKING CLOCK,
In Oak, Walnut, Mahogany, or Rosewood Cases, has 12 in. dial, goes 8
days, warranted. Gold Chains, Ladies' and Gents' 18 carat; Alberts,
Victorias, Fobs, &c.

SOLID SILVER ALBERTS & CHAINS.

Standard Gold Wedding Rings, and 18 carat gold keepers and guardrings.
Gold Brooches, Suits, Studs, Silver Links, Collar Buttons,
Pencils, Tooth Picks, and every other kind of Jewellery made.

ELECTRO PLATE AND NICKLE SILVER SPOONS & FORKS,
Warranted to wear like Silver for twenty years.

First-class Table Cutlery by Joseph Rodgers and Sons, and other
celebrated makers.

Writing Desks, Work Boxes, Dressing Cases, Jewel Cases, Tea Caddies,
Inkstands, &c., &c, OPTICIAN.

Agent for Laurence's celebrated Spectacles.

Above, by the 1870s Fattorini was advertising gold and silver jewellery; below, a diamond ring receipt from 1921

on the long balcony of the market, an area known as the Bazaar. He paid £18 a year for the lease. For the first time he was able to trade in quality jewellery, although he still needed to sell fancy goods to ensure his income. In 1831 he opened a shop at the 'Oriental Lounge', 14 Regent Parade, Harrogate, and in 1846 opened his first shop in Bradford at 28 Kirkgate.

They had eleven children, including eight sons, and the large family was a major factor in the success of the enterprise, helping on the stalls and in the shops. One son, Innocent, moved to Skipton to open his own shop as a working jeweller.

Antonio's youngest son, John, was to make the greatest contribution to a change in society, for he set out to put a watch into the pockets of every member of Bradford's working class population, an idea which led to the creation of Empire Stores, one of Britain's largest mail order companies. Until then watches had been hand-made and their prices were beyond what the average working person could afford, but in America the Waltham Watch Company of Boston began the mass production of watches and this led to the lowering of prices.

Watches previously costing several guineas were now superseded by ones costing a pound. This was still a week's wage for many of the poorer members of the community. But John had an idea how he could make it possible for even the poor to have a watch of their own – he started the Fattorini Watch Clubs! Every club had a chairman and a treasurer and members were called to a weekly meeting, usually in a pub, where they paid their sixpenny payment, continuing for a year. When the club's fund reached £1. 5s. (the price of a watch) a watch was purchased and raffled among the members. The winner had the watch, but was in effect buying his watch by weekly instalments, for he continued to pay his sixpence for the full 50 weeks. Eventually, through this method, all the club members owned their own silver pocket watch.

By using the Watch Club Fattorini was able to expand without having to acquire premises or take on large numbers of staff. By 1900 there were over 100 watch clubs throughout the country. Members were eventually allowed to have other goods, or a cheque that could only be spent in a Fattorini shop, and so the first mail order business began. Soon the firm started issuing catalogues and goods were sent to customers through the post. Cash from defaulters, and fines on late-payers went into a social fund, supplemented by discounts on goods given by Fattorini, and subsequently provided a supper at the end of the year. These social clubs were the foundation of the mail order giant.

The Ferodo Trophy made by Fattorini's

a competition to design the FA Cup. Originally valued at fifty guineas it was won for the first time, in 1911, by Bradford City. Since then Fattorini's have made the Rugby League Challenge Cup, motor racing's Ferodo Gold Trophy, and many other sporting awards.

Civic regalia is another Fattorini speciality and many town halls display wonderful items of silver designed and assembled in the Bradford workshops. Antonio Fattorini, of Harrogate, brother of Maria, supplied the Harrogate mayoral chain in 1884. When Field Marshal Montgomery was given the Freedom of Huddersfield the town presented him with a silver fruit-bowl made by Fattorini's.

Early in the century this aspect of the business had grown to the point that it became a separate concern, with premises in Sackville Street, Bradford. Fattorini tried to register the company as the Northern Trading Company but the Registrar of Companies refused to allow the name as it was already in use by another firm. The name 'Empire Stores' was registered.

At the same time Antonio Fattorini continued to develop as a jeweller and silversmith at 28 Westgate as well as in Kirkgate. Shortly before the Second World War the jewellery business moved to Tyrrel Street, Bradford, where it still operates today, although the Fattorini family still have the business in Parliament Street, Harrogate, through Maria Fattorini, daughter of the founder, who married into the Tindall family.

Before the turn of the century Fattorini's started manufacturing, and supplying, sporting trophies and regalia from the Bradford shop and in 1911 won

Today the firm is well respected throughout Yorkshire. The Bradford shop is now part of the the Goldsmith jewellery group, whilst the Harrogate shop is still owned by descendants of Antonio Fattorini.

Fattorini's shop in Westgate, Bradford, in the 1920s

Green Flag

In Hull in the late 1960s Dennis Thrustle offered locals a special holiday insurance scheme. For a payment of £1.50 anyone going on holiday in the British Isles could be assured that if their car broke down he would get them back home, although they would have to wait until Dennis arrived with his Landrover to tow them. This led to the formation in Hull of Auto Speed Recovery Service.

On a visit to Hull, Bradfordian Gordon Sheard Whitehead heard about this scheme and told Colin M R Wilkinson, a successful local businessman. Both thought the concept was brilliant and they decided to adapt it to their locality. They formed The National Breakdown Recovery Club in February 1971. They were joined by Jack Blyth, a local builder who was also Colin Wilkinson's brother-in-law.

Their first premises were at Claremont Garage in Morley Street, Bradford, and although they operated nationally they only recruited members locally. Towards the end of the year Gordon Sheard Whitehead left the company and his place was taken by Bob Slicer, who continued to run his two fish and chip shops and only served the company on a part-time basis.

Ernest Smith worked for the Auto Speed Recovery Service in the West Riding area, but when the parent company got into financial difficulties National Breakdown and Ernest got together to see if a rescue package could be put together. At that time the National Breakdown Recovery Club had about 9,000 members and an annual turnover of £12,500, with a membership fee of £1.50, but Ernest brought with him a further 30,000 members, mainly from West Yorkshire. Eventually Bob Slicer sold his fish and chip shops and became full time managing director and he and Ernest Smith worked closely together to develop the business which began to grow rapidly.

In June 1974 the Department of Trade and Industry caused the young company a major concern by deciding that they were carrying on an insurance business and, as the company was not underwritten, they must cease trading. However, although the DTI initially appeared to be a threat to their future in reality its staff were most helpful and suggested they contacted David Roberts at Fenchurch Re-insurance who in turn introduced them to Lloyds underwriters. The relationship proved very successful and lasted for several years.

The Civil Service Motoring Association signed a contract in 1976 with National Breakdown and this generated a huge increase in membership, so much so that by 1982 half the membership came from that Association. In 1977 the company bought a small insurance company, which had a turnover of only £30,000. It had been developed by Mike Davies and was called Ultra Keen Recovery; today it still underwrites all

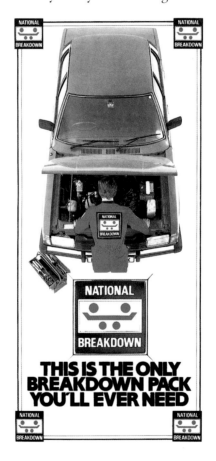

THIS IS THE ONLY BREAKDOWN PACK YOU'LL EVER NEED

their work under its more recognised company name UKI. In 1977 two non executive directors were appointed, Jeffrey Pittock and Harry Clough, both local businessmen who brought their considerable experience to the Board. In 1979 the company moved to larger premises at Low Moor, Bradford, which with continued expansion were soon fully occupied.

Bob Slicer retired from the company in January 1982 and Ernest Smith took over as Chief Executive but the next few months were not easy because the Civil Service Motoring Association decided to set up its own recovery service. This could have been the end of National Breakdown but due to the dedicated staff many members who could so easily have been lost were retained and the turnover of £2 million was also maintained.

A strong marketing team then ensured that the company received wider public recognition and a new marketing approach was made to National Car Parks to market the services through their car parks. This was an important move for eventually NCP offered to acquire the company, buying out the shareholders with the exception of Ernest Smith who stayed on as managing director.

The Gulf War was a time of concern, for if petrol rationing had come it could have destroyed the company and a decision was made to diversify. Already certain initiatives had been taken to help members who motored into Europe and Green Flag SA had been formed in Strasbourg. Similarly in the United States another firm had asked for permission to use the National Break-

down name there, and this had been agreed providing the company did not seek to expand into Britain or Europe. Home Assistance Services was also formed to offer people plumbing and other home care services in case of emergency. Was National Breakdown the right name? It was decid-

Alan Shearer, captain of the England football team, sponsored by Green Flag

ed that Green Flag was better, for it not only crossed borders between companies but could be an international symbol.

The decision was right for not only were they offered a stake in the American company but they bought Travellers Medical Service in 1990, to help those injured on holiday or by accidents on the Continent, and indeed worldwide; the name proved all embracing. A year earlier, in 1989, the Princess of Wales opened their purpose built offices in Pudsey, which employs over 1,000 employees. In 1982 the company's turnover was £2 million; in the current year this now fully international company has a turnover of £120 million.

Est^d 1860

GREENWOODS

James Greenwood was born in 1823 in Bradford and as a young man went to work for a Mr Stringer Lake who had a hatter's shop in the centre of Bradford, at 29 Westgate. In 1860 Stringer Lake disappeared and was never seen again!

James Greenwood acquired the shop and with the help of his son Moses, who was only twelve years old, developed the business. In 1865 the premises had to be demolished for road widening and James decided to give up hatting but Moses took a shop at 148 Westgate and carried on the business from there – Moses' brother Aaron took a shop at 104 Westgate in opposition.

Moses was not easily deterred; he would sit in his little shop, working by the light of a flickering gas jet, making hats for Bradford's wool barons. In 1889 he moved his business down the road to 142 Westgate and started making straw hats, although the fashionable silk hats were the backbone of his trade.

In 1894 Moses' son Willie Greenwood joined his father and eventually persuaded him that they should become outfitters. Willie used to jump on his carrier bike and ride the ten miles to the wholesalers, Holts, in Leeds to buy ties and braces, which he brought back to the shop. Later he introduced Union and Sateen shirts and stiff white collars. In 1903 Willie extended to the next door premises and a new shop front was installed by a firm called Newall, whose works manager was a Mr Sharp. Later Mr Sharp was joined by Mr Law and they founded the firm of Sharp & Law who remained Greenwood's shopfitters until 1989 when they ceased trading.

When Aaron retired in the early 1900s Willie took over. Although the shop did not open until 9am it did not close until 8pm on Monday to Thursday, remaining open until 10pm on Friday, and midnight on Saturday. There was no half day and the shop only closed on Sundays, Good Friday and Christmas Day.

Right, Moses Greenwood at work in the 1870s; below, sale time at Crown Street, Halifax, in 1953

The size of the shop increased again in 1921, giving them a corner site. The family lived over the shop and Walter Greenwood was born there in 1901; he joined the family firm in 1919 and was made a partner in 1922, along with his younger brothers Arthur and Harold. Walter opened a branch in London in 1925 but that venture was short lived.

In 1923 Walter Greenwood married Anne Nellist and they had two sons, Denis and Brian, who later became joint managing directors and co-chairmen. In 1927 Walter separated from his father and brothers and took charge of the branches whilst they retained the main shop and the warehouse. Walter's business expanded rapidly and soon he had shops in Sunderland, Middlesbrough, Darlington, Shipley and Heckmondwike; he was however still his own window-dresser, stocktaker and buyer! By 1932 he had 26 shops and when his father retired he took back the Westgate shop, using it as his headquarters. Harold continued to work for Walter but brother Arthur started a hat factory in Preston.

The business now became Greenwoods (Hosiers & Outfitters) Ltd. In 1933 they took over a dance hall in Drewton Street, Bradford, which became the head office and warehouse. A year later the shops totalled 36, although some of the smaller ones were eventually closed.

Soon after the Second World War, Denis and Brian Greenwood entered the business and in 1952 the company opened its 100th branch, in Huddersfield. A further major development came in 1956 when the company laid the foundation stones for its new head office and warehouse at White Cross, Guiseley, about 10 miles from Leeds and Bradford. As the company made various takeovers the number of shops rose to 200.

Willie Greenwood died in 1970, aged 91, and Walter died soon afterwards leaving Denis and Brian to carry on the business. In 1982 it was

What Greenwoods had on offer in June 1931

decided to divide the business into two sections; Denis retained the Greenwood shops whilst Brian took control of the shops which had been purchased under the Hodges name along with the property company, Shop & Store Developments Ltd, and a variety store in Wigan, named, 'Lowes'.

Over the years smaller and uneconomical shops have been closed, but most of the freeholds of the remaining 180 shops are owned by the company. They have had to respond to changes in the sale of menswear, including the development of out of town shopping centres and supermarkets who have their own clothing departments. Greenwoods continue, however, to hold major sites in many towns and cities throughout the country.

HAREWOOD

arewood is mentioned in the Domesday Book, when it belonged to three Saxon chieftains. During the Norman Conquest a Lascelles travelled with William the Conqueror, and the family have certainly been in Yorkshire since 1315 when John de Lascelles lived at Hinderskelfe, now known as Castle Howard.

In 1738 John Boulter sold Harewood estate to Henry Lascelles, and it has been owned by the Lascelles family ever since. The family in the 17th century acquired sugar plantations in Barbados, this being the principle source of the family fortunes which made the building of Harewood House possible.

Edwin Lascelles, Lord Harewood, was born in 1712, and he commissioned John Carr of York not only to design a house, but also stables and a 'model' village. Work on the stable block began in 1755. Edwin showed the plans of the development to Robert Adam, then an outstanding young architect, but little of Adam's changes can be seen on the exterior of the house, although the interior is regarded as one of his masterpieces. Robert Adam employed the finest craftsmen to paint decorative panels on the ceilings, to create remarkable plasterwork, and to supply furniture to complete the grand design. He chose Thomas Chippendale, who originated from nearby Otley, but whose work had become recognised and who now had a workshop in London, to design and construct furniture and furnishings for the whole house. This was his most elaborate commission, much of his work rivalling the very best work of French designers of the period.

In 1772 Capability Brown, one of the country's finest landscape designers came to Harewood and Lascelles commissioned him to transform the 1800 acre park in his naturalistic manner, working closely with nature. In contrast to the architect and interior designer, Capability Brown knew he would never see his work come to maturity; he was designing for future generations. Edwin Lascelles died at Harewood House in 1795, but as he had no direct heir, the estate passed to his cousin Edward Lascelles, Tory MP for Northallerton.

Edward, Viscount Lascelles, painted by Hoppner

Edward Lascelles, 1st Earl of Harewood, and his eldest son, also Edward, added greatly to the collection of portraits. Edward, Viscount Lascelles, was a friend of Turner and Girtin and a patron of the arts, bringing to Harewood the collection of Chinese celadon and French porcelain. Viscount Lascelles died before his father, and was succeeded by his brother Henry, who was in turn succeeded by his son, also Henry. This Henry married Lady Louisa Thynne and they had 13 children. Louisa's family home was Longleat and perhaps because of their large family and possibly because she missed her ancestral home she called in Sir Charles Barry, the architect of the Houses of Parliament, to enlarge and alter Harewood House. Sir Charles added a third storey, swept away the classical portico on the south facade and added the massive terrace. Inside the house, rooms were altered and some of Adam's work was substantially changed – the early Victorians were no respecters of the past.

The 6th Earl of Harewood received a considerable inheritance from the 2nd Marquess of Clanricarde, and he used substantial sums for fine Italian pictures. He married Princess Mary, who in 1932 was created Princess Royal by her father King George V, and they embarked on restoration and refurbishment.

From early in its history visitors have been taken round Harewood by the house-keeper. Early in the 19th century a guide book was published and today the house is frequently used for public occasions. In 1947 many treasures had to be sold by the family to pay heavy death duties, but Harewood House is still rich with its art collections, fine buildings, and landscape.

A social change was taking place and the big landowners were being forced to sell off parts of their estates, often putting at risk a unity of landscape and building, as well as community, which had been built up over centuries. At Harewood there was much to be done following the war years, but crippling death duties of £800,000 on an estate then valued at £1.4 million were horrendous and in 1950 and 1951 sales of land mounted to 14,600 acres; by the mid 1960s what had been an estate of 24,000 acres only a few years before, was now only 7000 acres. Lord Harewood realised that things would not return to the pre-war situation and believed that such historic country houses could become an asset which the public could share.

1950 saw the first paying visitors arrive at Harewood House, although they could only see five state apartments – the Rose Drawing Room, the Green Drawing Room, the Gallery, the Dining Room and the Music Room. Harewood was an immediate success. The family moved to a new suite of apartments on the first floor, looking out on the north front; in future the family and the public would co-exist in harmony, at least for the most part!

In 1970 the now famous Harewood Bird Garden was opened as a visitor attraction; more recently the Terrace Gallery and the Adventure Playground have been added. By 1972 the number of visitors had risen to an amazing 263,000.

Today the estate is run by the Harewood House Trust. The Bird Garden is home to some 120 species of exotic bird, many being regarded as vulnerable to extinction in their native habitat. Harewood is also an educational centre, being host to numerous events, but also used to encourage the young to take an active interest in conservation and the countryside. For the businessman or woman the estate is the venue for important conferences and corporate din-

Harewood House, South Front

ners; for the enthusiast it is the annual location for specialist rallies, outdoor concerts, or exhibitions. For the music lover the chamber concerts in the Gallery, started by the present Earl of Harewood and his wife in the late 1960s, are a rare opportunity to hear world class players in ideal surroundings. The impressive gardens are continually being renewed and several areas will, it is hoped, be restored to their former glory as funds become available.

SONOCO
HARLANDS

Edward Robinson Harland, the founder of what is today Sonoco Harland, was initially indentured to a grocer, but the following year he changed his mind and became indentured to a printer. After completing his apprenticeship he started his own business and a Hull directory for 1835 lists him as a Bookbinder at 2 Prospect Street. Three years later, obviously expanding, he is listed as a Printer, Bookbinder and Stationer at 11 Carlisle Street. This was the year of his 'Registration as a Printer', a necessary procedure in those days.

Sadly Edward Harland died in 1844 leaving Mary, his widow, with five children and the responsibility of carrying on the business. Little is known of the next few years but they must have been hard in many ways. Later his son, Edward, wrote of his mother that she "was

Above, Edward R Harland and right, his son Edward

a woman of rare courage and ability and succeeded in keeping the business together where ninety-nine out of a hundred women would have broken down under similar circumstances." By 1863 the business had become known as M. Harland & Son, the initial 'M' indicating that Mary was in charge. She traded as a Printer & Stationer at 14 Carlisle Street, although the printing was done at 32 Scale Lane. Carlisle Street was an ideal location for a printer and stationer for apparently it had a variety of businesses, including a Music Seller, Clock & Watch repairer, Painter & Grainer, Boot

& Shoe Maker, Confectioner, Plumber & Glazier, and a Milliner & Corset maker – all would need printing and stationery.

Edward Harland jnr entered the business in his early teens and at once his energy revitalized it. Following a disastrous fire at the Scale Lane premises in 1865 they built a new printing works in Manor Street, in an area known as the Land Of Green Ginger, where 'Green Ginger' used to grow in the time of King Henry.

Over the next 20 years adjacent land was bought and in 1886 a building three times the size of the original one was built and equipped. On 4th January 1887 a 'festive gathering' was held to celebrate the opening of this three-storey building, which had a ground area of 1000 square yards, at the "Phoenix" Printing Works of Messrs. M. Harland & Son at Manor Street, Land of Green Ginger. The building had been decorated with greenery and mottoes, there was a celebration tea and the event concluded with an entertainment of songs and recitations.

This was the first time that the word "Phoenix" was used in relation to the company. No doubt the legend of the fabulous bird which built a funeral pile of wood and aromatic gum, lit it with the fanning of its wings, and then rose from the flames with renewed life inspired the name for the new printing works.

Visitors were shown round the amazing range of new machinery, some of which had been patented by Edward Harland. In those early days one of the common lines printed by the firm was tickets for pawnbrokers. It is said that Frederick Harland, Mary's grandson, knew almost every pawnbroker in the country; they were divided into different areas, each area having its own special form of ticket.

Gradually M. Harland's became known for its expertise in the specialist printing work known as "Numerical Printing", when rolls of tickets were produced, each ticket being printed, numbered in sequence, and perforated in one operation. These tickets were in great demand for use on trams, ferryboats, cinemas, etc. Other specialised work was the theatre ticket where each one had to be unique, relating to one specific seat in the theatre for one specific performance.

When the work was at its prime, in the inter-war period, Harland's were producing about 70% of all such tickets used nationally. When Harry Harland, Frederick's brother, was at the helm he printed almost every type of ticket imaginable, but drew back at the idea of producing tickets for dog-racing, being a staunch Methodist. Even today Harlands are one of only a few firms capable of producing such numerical tickets, but generally they have been superseded by computer generated tickets.

Frederick Harland, who succeeded his father Edward, was a man of vision and played a major role in the company for about 70 years – he died in 1956 aged 86, still chairman of the company.

The Second World War brought difficult times for the business. Situated in the centre of Hull, the directors realised the firm was vulnerable to enemy action, particularly when Hull received very heavy bombings, and it was decided to transfer the works to Pocklington. An unused cinema was found to house the equipment and staff travelled from Hull each day by train, whilst the directors walked to the factory, and the boilerman made tea for the 'fire-watchers'.

After the war when a Labour government was elected, the directors thought their investment might suffer. They favoured Frederick Harland's idea of opening a subsidiary company in South Africa, where many old colonial values were still held. Matthew Calvert had worked in India selling fire extinguishers, but now set up the printing unit in an old prisoner of war camp in Marisberg. This venture lasted for some 20 years, but when political change came in South Africa, the directors accepted an offer and broke the link. At one time they ventured into France but, finding the business environment not to their

Above, a selection of Harland's printed material; right, Harland is one of few printers specialising in perforated numbered tickets

liking, quickly severed the connection. Bill Morrison married Mary Harland, and subsequently joined the company, becoming a director of the firm, along with Edward Harland. Bill had an eye for colour and beauty, and felt that numerical printing was boring. Looking for other outlets for their work he came across Seal presses. Here a reel of foil was pressed with a steel dye which had an embossed surface; the resulting embellishment to the package sold well, surprisingly, on kipper packs at the docks. These labels proved most popular and soon there was a great demand for them from many other people.

At the 1953 Coronation of Queen Elizabeth II, Harlands had won the rights to print coronation seals, and this type of seal soon found its way into packaging for the cosmetic industry with Helena Rubinstein, Revlon, Rimmel and Elizabeth Arden. At this time most of the work came from other parts of the country rather than from Hull where they had no representatives, perhaps thinking that local people would beat their own path to their door.

The company's next major development was the pressure sensitive label, otherwise known as the self-adhesive label. It was a major technical challenge to be able to cut through the first layer of the label, without cutting into the backing sheet. These labels were particularly valuable to the pharmaceutical industry, offering a much higher degree of adhesion and security as the labels were held on a reel and fixed to the container whilst it was still in the plant. Although they were small runs they were of high value. The company established its own design studio and this new expertise culminated in the creation of the Beverley based subsidiary Trident, which works with many multinationals managing and developing the graphics for many of their global brands.

As new packaging materials, such as polythene and polystyrene have been developed, new processes and new adhesives have become necessary to ensure that labels on frozen products and new substrates remain firmly fixed. Similarly new developments have taken place in printing ink technology, particularly where inks can now be 'cured', using ultra violet rays, rather than being left to dry.

In the early 1970s a subsidiary company was set up in Salford to produce machines which would give good security and enable the labels to be applied in the factory where the product was packed. Customers at that time, as today, include The Body Shop, Procter & Gamble, and suppliers to Marks & Spencer.

In 1994 Harlands become part of the American Sonoco group with Ian Ross as chief executive; he is now succeeded by David Hewitt, formerly sales and marketing director.

On the grave of the Harland family are these words by Burke: "People will never look forward to posterity who never look backward to their ancestors."

Top, Harlands printed special embossed gold labels to mark the Queen's 50th anniversary; above another example of embossing, this time for Christmas gifts

Kenyon Sons & Craven Ltd was formed in Rotherham in 1853; in 1891 it became a limited liability company manufacturing sugar confectionery, jams and pickles at a factory in Morpeth Street, Rotherham, with another factory in Hull. Over many of the early years trading was difficult and between 1900 and 1904 the directors took no remuneration! However by 1917 the company was doing well, but in 1931 they sold the Hull factory; it took two years to sell, and then they only received £3,000 for it. The sad situation continued until 1943 when the directors resigned.

By 1943 Simon Heller had become chairman of Kenyon Sons & Craven Ltd at a time when it had only 50 employees left, but he was a young tough chairman, determined to succeed. Gradually he moved the company into the nut business, building on his previous experience operating his own Hercules Nut Company in London and Leeds. In 1947 Simon Heller had a small room for an office, which he shared with Owen Pilley, the company secretary, and Bill Leek, who was responsible for the works. Bill told later how Simon never encouraged anyone to sit – he wanted producers, not paper-pushers!

There are many such tales of those early days, of how the company made sweets, and also of how it had an arrangement with a trader in Sheffield Vegetable Market who 'tipped' them off when there was a glut. A van would go to the market, collect whatever was cheap and bring it back to the factory to be made into chutney or similar products. New machinery was also unobtainable but a small second-hand gas frying-machine was bought and used to cook small allocations of nuts. In 1948 hazelnuts became available; these were roasted, salted and delivered to shops and cinemas.

The firm moved to Rotherham's Eastwood Trading Estate in 1950, and Simon still gave his all, often taking paperwork home in the evening. No order was ever turned away. The company supplied Bassetts with ground coco-

Top, one of the early Hercules packs; above, a 1951 letter from Kenyon Son and Craven selling their Transparent packets of roasted and salted almonds

nut, although they had to learn how to grind it as they went along. When sugar was scarce Simon Heller set up a factory in Barbados to make sugar syrup to send to Britain, but as sugar became available he phased out the pickling and concentrated on peanuts.

Simon Heller realised that 2d was a psychological price for a packet of peanuts and in 1953 he introduced the twopenny packet of 'KP Nuts', the first nationally distributed line in nuts and the first use of the brand name 'KP' – he took the

This 1965 letterhead shows how the products range had developed

initials from Kenyon Produce.

As the nuts took over – peanuts, cashews or almonds – so other products were gradually phased out. Nuts were roasted or salted and were also sold as mixed fruit and nuts; the customers loved them and demand grew. Changes brought improvements in quality and production, continuous frying raised output to two tons per hour; Maurice Cohen, a former chief development engineer at Rowntrees, had joined KP Nuts in 1956, and it was his unique technological skills that enabled the firm to progress at such a remarkable pace. At the beginning of the 1960s KP Nuts occupied a lowly place in the market, at the end of the decade they were the market leader.

To ensure that KP had the best nuts available, staff went to Uganda, Malawi and Tanganyika – now Tanzania, a country famous for the notorious Ground Nuts Scheme.

In 1962 Marks & Spencer asked KP to produce packs of St. Michael nuts, and fruit with nuts. Michael Heller, Simon's son, took personal charge of the account and built up a close relationship with the firm, who passed on technological experience to KP, such as date-coding on the inner and outer cartons and on the packets. The nuts had a shelf life of about ten weeks, but KP were market leaders by agreeing to take stock back and give credit notes, thereby ensuring that stock on the shelves was always of the highest quality.

Between 1964 and 1966 KP doubled the size of their factory, before its sale to United Biscuits in 1968 when it had a turnover of £5 million. Michael Heller, although only 32, joined the board of United Biscuits and remained as managing director of KP Nuts until the end of 1970. Simon Heller became a legend in his lifetime; he may have driven his staff, but they respected him for his energy, his enthusiasm, and his great abilities – he created an industry!

In 1971 KP Nuts, with its 1500 staff, became part of United Biscuits Foods Division. In 1962 production had been 8 hundredweights an hour, by 1971 it had reached 7 tons an hour. Today KP still dominates the British nut market and exports products from Rotherham to other European countries. It is by far the largest United Kingdom processor of nut products and intends to continue building on the firm foundations set by Simon Heller.

Samuel Cunliffe Lister was born at Calverley Hall, between Leeds and Bradford, but when he was a young boy they moved to the family seat, Manningham Hall in Bradford, where Samuel lived for more than half a century.

As one of the younger sons of an aristocratic family it was traditional that Samuel would enter the church as a profession! But Samuel had other ideas and he went to work in a counting house in Liverpool and made several trips to America. He was impressed with what he saw and came back with stories of large capital investments; his admiration for the 'Yankees' was such that he became known as 'American Sam'.

At the end of his apprenticeship he went into partnership with his brother, John Cunliffe Lister, as a spinner and manufacturer in the rural hamlet of Manningham. John had previously had a mill in Bradford. Together they took possession of a new mill built for them by their father. It was a difficult time and John left after two years, inherited the family properties and became a wealthy man.

Dr. Edmund Cartwright had taken out a patent for wool-combing machinery as early as 1790, but experiments were

Centre, Samuel Cunliffe Lister; right, an artist's impression of part of Manningham Mills in the 1880s

still going on to develop a more effective machine; Samuel Lister favoured the work of George Donisthorpe. Lister had limitless funds to invest in the development of the machine; he also had tremendous energy, which he gave freely. The resultant machine not only did the work more quickly but also caused less damage to the wool and the combing was more complete. It was highly profitable – but soon there were no hand-combers!

Once Lister had mastered wool-combing he moved to new ventures. On visiting a warehouse in London he noticed a heap of 'rubbish' in a corner, and was told it was waste silk, which was unusable and therefore sold as rubbish. Samuel never accepted the word 'impossible'; it simply meant there was something to conquer. He offered the owner a half-penny a pound for it and the owner was pleased to see it go. For the next eight years, up to 1865, he worked to convert

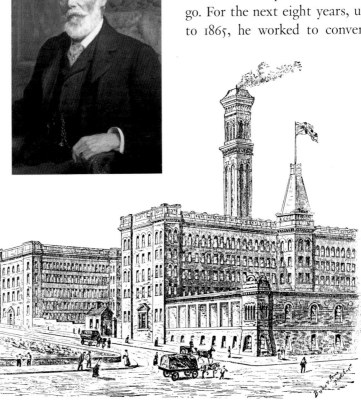

this material into a valuable resource. He then went on to invest in silk farms in Assam and later the Punjab; when the Assam venture proved unsuccessful he turned the land into successful tea plantations. Altogether he registered 150 patents, more than any other man in England; the cost brought even Lister near to bankruptcy.

In 1853 Samuel Lister inherited the estate at Manningham. The grounds of the Manningham

One of the silk weaving departments at Manningham Mills in 1918 below, burling and mending of George Aked worsted materials at Manningham Mills in 1962

estate were well wooded and extended to about 50 acres. At Whitsuntide each year, before Bradford had any other parks, he threw open his estate to local people, made a small charge, and gave the proceeds to charities.

When in 1870 he moved to Farfield Hall at Addingham he sold the estate and the hall to Bradford Corporation for £40,000. The estate was renamed Lister Park and on the site of the family home was built Cartwright Hall, to which Lister contributed £50,000, as a personal tribute to Edmund Cartwright.

Fire destroyed the mill in 1871, but larger premises were built on the same site, the frontage along Heaton Road extending to a quarter of a mile, the total area being about 17 acres. The mill's dominant feature was its huge stone chimney which is still a local landmark. Built in an Italian campanile style it is about 250 feet high and has a foundation four feet thick and which covers 40 square feet; it weighs 8,000 tons! At the mill's opening in 1873 Lister climbed to the top of the chimney and drank a glass of champagne to celebrate its completion.

Listers mill became synonymous with the production of velvets. In 1889 the company was converted into a joint-stock company with a share capital of £1,550,000. Already they were world leaders in the production of velvets, silks, imitation sealskins, and mohair-plush; they wove woollen-dress goods, nightwear, men's shirtings and pyjamas, and sewing-silks. Two thirds of their sales were for export. By now Samuel Lister was a multi-millionaire owning several estates in the county, and in 1891 he became Lord Masham. The mill at Manningham consumed 50,000 tons of coal each year so

Listers bought their own colliery at Pontefract and also about this time acquired mills in Nuneaton to gain further silk production capacity.

The years immediately following Samuel Lister's death in 1906 were difficult trading years. Although people discovered the durability of silk, they found its costs high and sometimes remade garments to meet changing fashions; often material had to be sold at a much lower profit margin. The death of Edward VII brought some respite as people wanted mourning outfits – and then further new outfits for the coronation of the new monarch; Lister & Co.were commissioned to make 1,000 yards of wide width velvet for draping Westminster Abbey at the express wish of King George V and Queen Mary, who had earlier toured the mill.

Soon the looms took on a more serious purpose – providing material for military use. Britain was at war with Germany, one of its main export markets. Many staff left to take up arms, some, sadly, never to return. Until 1917 Listers had depots in all the principal Russian towns but when the Communist Revolution came, money in their banks was lost forever.

After the war, business was better than ever before, but prosperity was short lived, and the Great Depression of the early 1920s followed.

Listers also joined with J & P Coats to build a factory in Sao Paulo, Brazil to manufacture sewing-silks, and became suppliers of hand-knitting yarns which were used by thousands of war-widows, 'Listers Lavenda' being very popular.

In the early 1930s they introduced the trade name 'Dreadnought', for velvets for theatre seating, and there was a demand for goat-hair furnishings and for Lister moquette to upholster Morris cars which were pouring off the production lines at Cowley. They also made simulated animal skins and furs, and 'Casket Plush', exported to the United States, for coffin linings.

As early as 1938 the storm clouds were again appearing on the horizon and the following year Listers were making a major contribution to the war effort. They produced, among other things, 1,180 miles of nylon parachute fabric, 1,330 miles of real silk parachute, 4,430 miles of parachute cord made from nylon and silk and 1,440 miles of shell cloth. They also made special camouflage cloth, which was then covered with rubber and inflated into the shape of a tank or a military truck!

After the war there was a surge in demand, but a shortage of skilled workers. Across in

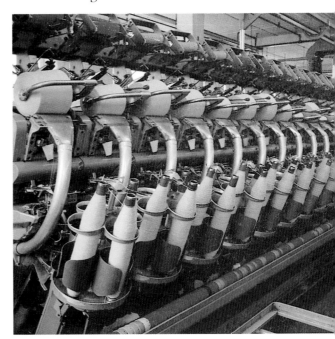

Some of the modern equipment used by Joseph Hoyle & Son. This is a Savio cone-winder with automatic electronic yarn-clearing system

Barrow-in-Furness, although there was work for men in the shipyard, there was little for women to do. Listers promptly erected a building there, took machinery from Bradford and Addingham mills and quickly trained staff, starting production of hand-knitting wools. Back in Bradford, in 1947, heavy snowfalls brought operations to a standstill; near

Addingham mills there were snow-drifts over 12 feet deep!

There were other mills in Bradford with a long history, among them George Aked's, founded in 1869. It had been bought in 1944 by Eugene Kornberg and John Segal, known throughout the trade as 'K&S'. Aked's had branched out and were using several types of loom which gave them great flexibility in cloth production. While Listers stayed with wool, K&S, at Aked's, were manufacturing new fabrics made from synthetic products, including blends of wool and terylene which became popular with Marks & Spencer, and Burtons. Soon K&S were receiving large orders for these new materials from the RAF.

Towards the end of the 1950s Listers became the focus of stock market interest,

and in May 1959 it was recommended that shareholders accept a bid by Eugene Kornberg and John Segal, directors of a group of spinning and manufacturing companies.

Soon K & S had executive control and revival was in hand. Their new managing director was dynamic Wilfred Asquith; there was new vision, they were entrepreneurs. One new fabric, Minquilla, won the Fur Fabric Division Queen's Award for Exports in 1971, attracting new business from Russia. The group was involved in every kind of yarn, with the exception of carpeting; as more companies were added they operated 23 mills. Through the Aked arm of the group Listers were one of the initial seven British licensees for Crimplene.

In 1973 Listers were awarded a Royal Warrant for furnishing fabrics, although they were feeling the effects of the Arab oil price war. Once again the time had come for change, only now it would be contraction, under the guidance of the new chief executive, Michael Dracup, with staffing levels falling from 4,200 to 1,600! The whole textile industry was in crisis. Listers had created several new slim-line businesses; they were determined to succeed and by 1987 their turnover had increased to £50 million, with profits of £3.25 million.

Today Listers velvets are still manufactured at Manningham and are to be found in many celebrated places in the world, such as the White House in Washington and the Royal Opera House in Covent Garden, London. Bradford, and the British textile industry, has to compete with developing countries, but there are those who will always seek the specialist quality materials produced from companies such as Listers.

Left, Manningham Mills still dominates the Bradford skyline

The Duxbury family have lived in Bingley since the early 1700s and in the 1850s Thomas Duxbury had a greengrocer's shop near the Parish Church. Later his son Robert had a shop in Mornington Road.

Tom Duxbury inherited the business from Robert, and in 1907 he sold it to his second wife's father for about £7,000. Tom, a keen Baptist, used some of the money to visit the Holy Land but on his return to Bingley, the story is told, he swapped a horse for the Magnet Firelighting Co!

In addition to the greengrocery business, Robert Duxbury had built six houses in Whitley Street and one of these became the office for the new enterprise. During the First World War Tom earned a living by selling firelighters and firewood, the wood coming from barges which he dismantled and chopped up.

Tom and his wife had eight children. They were sent to Belle Vue Grammar School in Bradford to ensure they had a good education, but sadly their eldest son, Robert, was killed in action in 1916. It therefore came to Harry and John to run the business, but Harry died at the early age of 38 in 1943.

After the war the firm started buying and selling Government surplus stock, including boxes used to carry shells, bombs and similar items. Some of these they converted into hen huts and garden furniture before, in the early 1920s, they started to make windows and other joinery items for local builders. By the early 1930s the works in Whitley Street comprised a staircase up to the roof of the building, with three rooms on the first floor, an enquiry office, a general office, and a larger room for the three directors. Much of the production was manufacturing joinery for local authorities, but as builders could not work in winter it was either 'feast or famine'. Tom and his sons realised that the large contracts for authorities such as Walsall involved making windows and doors of regular sizes and from being a 'bespoke' joinery company they became a company which issued a catalogue of standard items.

At this time the company was under-capitalised and an appointment was made for Tom Duxbury and the company secretary to discuss the situation with the manager of the local Martins Bank, Mr. Hindle. After the secretary had explained the situation Mr. Hindle leaned forward and in a quiet voice said: "Well Mr. Duxbury, how much do you want?" Similarly Tom Duxbury leaned forward and replied,

Left to right, Harry, Tom and John Duxbury

"Well, Mr. Hindle, how much have you got?" They came away, after much laughter, with the overdraft raised to £4,500!

In 1936 the business was floated on the stock exchange, the family retaining a controlling interest. Expansion came quickly; a door factory was opened at Grays in Essex and a branch was created in Birmingham. Tom Duxbury was never a joiner, always a businessman, but when other joiners went to the toilet for a quick smoke, the 'No Smoking' policy was brought into action as a bucket of water was quickly

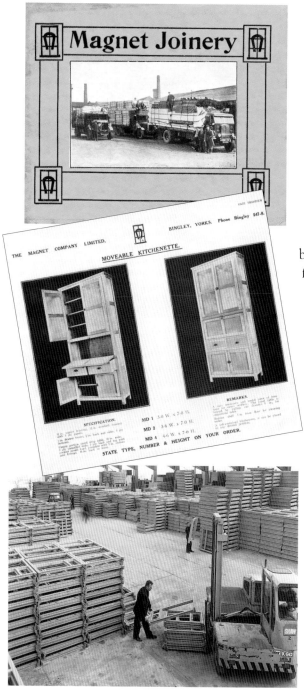

Top, the cover of an early Magnet brochure, and centre, one of the products advertised inside; above a Magnet warehouse in the 1970s

thrown over the toilet door!

After the Second World War Magnet gained contracts to supply timber components for developments in Sunderland, Liverpool and Birmingham whilst individual builders could continue to buy from their stock catalogue at varying discounts, thereby cutting out the builders-merchants while Magnet retained the merchants' profit margins.

By 1962 Magnet had opened 12 depots spread around the country. 1964 saw the company attain a profit of £1 million for the first time, but the following year this profit level had been doubled. Finding the Bingley Council unhelpful, Magnet built a new factory in Keighley and also bought the firm of William Brown in Darlington to give more production capacity.

In 1970 a new factory was built at Darlington, and by selling in large quantities, offering such a wide range of products, and having products available from stock, the operation became self-financing. They expanded their product range further by buying cupboards and patio doors from other suppliers until orders reached the size whereby they could justify building specialist facilities to manufacture their own. 'Service from Stock' became the Magnet motto.

Following the merger with Southern Evans in 1975 the company expanded to 250 depots. Magnet continued to be controlled by members of the Duxbury family until 1990.

In 1993 Berisford acquired Magnet from shareholders, including British banks, following the failure of what at that time had been the largest management buyout in United Kingdom commercial history. Berisford has since that time brought the company back into profitability and enabled it to become the number one joinery company in the United Kingdom. Today it brings to the customer new designs from around the world, and once again Magnet has become one of the country's most successful kitchen manufacturers.

William Marr was born in Dundee in 1808 but left Scotland to settle in Hull when he was a young man, having found work as a harpooner in the whaling industry. In Hull William, a fine young man who was 6' 3" tall, met and married Rachel Wood whose parents owned the Masons Arms public house in Chapel Lane, off Lowgate. After their marriage, William and Rachel also lived there.

Whaling was difficult and dangerous; it involved working in bad weather conditions and there were high losses of both men and ships. The 1835-36 whaling season was particularly disastrous and William died at sea and was buried in Greenland. On 16th October 1835 Rachel, a 21 year old widow, gave birth to William's son, and named him Joseph.

In 1841 Rachel married again, and William Elder, a fish merchant, became Joseph's stepfather; they moved to live at 6 Alfred Street, Hull.

When Joseph was 18 he went to Australia to make his fortune, working in Ballerat's gold fields, but later he returned to Hull and fell in love with Ann Stephenson.

Joseph had learned fish curing from his stepfather and in 1860 he rented two smoking kilns in the Dairycoates district of Hull and started his own business. The venture was a success and soon he purchased his own curing houses. In 1862 he married Ann – he was 27 and she was 19 – and bought their first home in St. Mark's Square, later moving to Vauxhall Grove, Hessle Road, which was nearer the business.

As the business grew Joseph diversified. He bought a newly-built fishing smack which he named Adelaide, expressing his continued love for Australia. Over the next 15 years he bought a further six new vessels, five of which were named after Joseph and Ann's daughters; he also added two second-hand smacks, an investment of several thousand pounds.

Joseph and Ann had 11 children, five girls and six boys, but three of these died in childhood. Their eldest son Joseph Arthur was set up in business as a fish curer by his father. By the 1870s the family had moved to 35 Nile Street, a select area of

The busy transport area of St Andrew's Dock in the 1930s. During this era an average of 350 railway fish vans would leave the dock each working day in eight special express freight trains

the city, and it was from here that the business was run; the dining room served as an office and the crews came to the house about every nine or ten weeks to receive their payments.

In the summer the smacks fished in fleets, their catches being taken to markets by fast sailing smacks, whereas in winter the smacks fished singly, trips averaging 14 – 21 days. Back at port the fish was sold by auction at the Hull market, under the supervision of the smack owner. The port was at its peak in 1887 when 448 smacks fished from Hull. Many smack owners were local men but others came from Brixham.

Fish laid out for auction on Fleetwood fish market

By the early 1890s Joseph's health had deteriorated, due to the strain of his hard life, and James Herbert Marr, their third son, gave up dentistry and he and his mother took over the running of the business. When steam-powered trawlers entered service some smack owners felt the new vessels would never replace the smacks, possibly because the operating costs of the steam-powered ones were higher. However Joseph and James had built their first steam trawler in 1891, naming it Marrs, and gradually all the other smacks were replaced; by 1903 the whole of the Hull smack fleet had gone.

In 1898 James moved to Fleetwood, taking with him some of the seagoing and shore staff, and three steam trawlers. Over the next few years the company expanded and now Joseph was

able to retire to Bridlington. Joseph died in 1900 and the firm remained a partnership between James and his mother until 1902 when it became a limited company, J Marr & Son Limited.

It was traditional to catch cod and haddock but James also developed a market for hake. In 1906 he diversified into curing, salting and fish merchanting, and along with James Robertson, formed the Lancashire Steam Fishing Co Ltd. James also helped found the Fylde Ice Company which supplied crushed ice for preserving fish. About this time he was joined, from Hull, by his brother Joseph Arthur. By 1913 the company had 32 trawlers but on the outbreak of war many were requisitioned by the government as mine sweepers or to provide armed escort.

In 1916 James Marr died, aged 47, and in 1919 following demobilisation, his son Alan took a place on the board, which had been held temporarily by his mother. The years following the First World War were particularly difficult for the company, for several directors died in a very short span, including 29 year old Alan Marr, James' son. Joseph Arthur Marr now became chairman, with Leslie and Geoffrey, James' twin sons, on the board. Geoffrey succeeded Joseph Arthur as chairman in 1929.

During the 1930s hake fishing on the west coast became barely profitable and it was decided to return to their home port of Hull and to fish off Bear Island. The company purchased the City Steam Fishing Company in 1934 and after an absence of 36 years returned to Hull. They continued to operate from Fleetwood and kept it as their major base; in 1939 they had 21 vessels at Fleetwood and 8 at Hull. In the Second World War the company lost its offices on St Andrew's Dock and also 29 vessels. Across at Fleetwood they became agents for widespread purchases of foreign fish.

After the war the company took delivery of

several new vessels, re-opened the Hull operation, and both Leslie and Geoffrey moved back to live in the city. Early in the 1950s the company purchased three diesel engined, three-deck bridge trawlers, each 190 feet long, at a total cost of almost £400,000! This was, however, the period when the Icelandic government imposed its four mile, and later twelve mile, fishing limits which brought the 'Cod War' with its difficult relationships. The company was now recognised as the largest privately owned British fish-trade business – its activities ranged from catching and landing fish to owning fish and chip shops!

In 1962 the company launched the first of its freezer trawlers, able to freeze the whole of its catch at sea, up to 25 tonnes a day in vertical plate freezers, with storage for up to 300 tonnes. To process the fish, once it had been landed, a new purpose-built factory was built in Walcott Street, Hull, which included a patented thawing machine. In 1968 J Marr & Son extended its operations to include Aberdeen.

During the 1970s the company embarked on a multi-million pound ship building programme, at a time when fish prices rose substantially but other costs made profit levels very low. Diversification was needed as foreign governments imposed further fishing restrictions and in 1972 they started to provide 'standby vessels' to offer emergency evacuation from North Sea oil wells; by 1982 14 of the company's vessels were used in this way.

1975 saw the closure of St Andrew's Dock, the home of the Hull fishing industry since 1883; it was replaced by the new purpose-built Albert Dock. That year almost saw the end of British deep sea fishing as Iceland imposed a 200 mile exclusion zone. The company's diversification policy now had to be further extended. One venture was the formation of J Marr (Seafoods)

Ltd, to buy mackerel from United Kingdom trawler owners and export it to West Africa, an operation which in 1980 gained the company the Queen's Award for Export.

Other Marr vessels became available for oil exploration work in the North Shetland and Norwegian Sea areas, for work on fishery protection for the Scottish Office, and for seismic work. During the Falklands War vessels were requisitioned to serve as minesweepers, and this led to the company developing an interest in

New diesel trawlers of the 1950s being fitted out at Princes Dock, Hull

fishing those waters in association with the Japanese Kanega (KSG) Association. Other projects have included work on the location of mineral deposits and earthquake faults off America's Pacific coast, managing the weather ship Cumulus for the Meteorological Office, and helping other companies with the design and specification of new ships.

J Marr Limited has moved a long way from William Marr's early activity as a harpooner on a whaler, but it has kept pace as the industry of the sea has changed, decade by decade.

Ogden
Of Harrogate Ltd

Charles and Ellen Ogden lived in Leeds with sons Walter and James Roberts Ogden. James was born in 1866 and a year later the family moved to Harrogate where Charles traded as a grocer at 4 Chapel Street (now Oxford Street).

In 1841 the Improvement Commissioners assigned land for development in what is today known as Parliament Street, Station Parade, Cambridge Street and Cambridge Crescent, and about seven years later Charles Ogden moved his business from Chapel Street into this fine curving block of new premises. He was prospering for instead of living above the premises, as many did, he bought a house in Oak Terrace. Between there and Cold Bath Road were a number of small quarries which supplied stone for the

development and, surprisingly, stones of quartz appeared in the soil, of such quality that they became known as 'Harrogate Diamonds'. Maybe these were the start of James' fascination with gem stones, for when he left school he became apprenticed to John Greenhalgh, who had a business in the newly-built market. Here he learned not only about precious stones, jewellery and about the making of clocks and watches, but also the importance of understanding his customers.

When Charles Ogden died in 1891 the estate was divided between his widow, Ellen, and his two sons. James combined his share of his father's money with his savings and in 1893 opened a shop at 23 Cambridge Street. His first recorded sale was a 'hall clock', sold for £2.12.6d. Soon he was selling brooches, chains, earrings, musical boxes and clocks. Among his customers was a Mr. Bennett, to whom he sold a pocket watch. Mr. Bennett was unable to pay outright and James allowed him to leave a deposit and take the watch away, paying the remainder week by week. Long before the payments were complete, on one of his weekly visits, Mr. Bennett was called in to see Mr. Ogden, who told him that further payment would not be necessary, as he had shown his watch to so many friends who had then become customers. This was typical of J R Ogden's generosity.

In 1897 the Little Diamond Shop enlarged as it took in adjoining premises. The family now included four sons and a daughter. When the Kursaal, the present Royal Hall, opened in 1903 to provide high class

Centre, J R Ogden; the company founder; left, the James Street premises

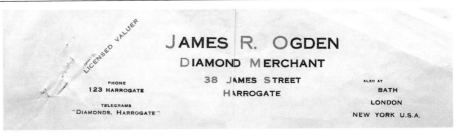

Right, a company letterhead from 1916; below right, an advertisement from the Yorkshire Homes Magazine of May 1927

entertainment, J R Ogden opened a shop in nearby Parliament Street to attract the new passing trade. Further shops were opened, at 7 Cambridge Crescent and at 33 Station Square, which he called the 'Little Watch Shop', complementing his 'Little Diamond Shop'. Further afield, shops were opened in Bath, Llandrindod Wells and Scarborough.

When Marshall & Snelgrove moved into fashionable James Street in 1906, they took a short tenancy of No 38 before moving to larger premises in the same street, J R Ogden took up the lease on No. 38 – a wise investment! He closed the premises in Station Square and erected an elegant canopy outside his fine new shop.

In 1913 the Lord Mayor of London, Sir David Burnett, made a special visit to Harrogate to officially open the new annex to the Royal Pump Room. The celebrations were quite magnificent and the State Landau, brought specially from London, drove along James Street, under a banner that James Ogden had ordered for the occasion, proclaiming "WELCOME – TO LONDON ON THE MOORS". That evening, in the Hotel Majestic, there was a magnificent banquet at which the Lord Mayor paid tribute to the town and those who were guiding its development; J R Ogden was among those gathered there.

The war was a tragedy in many different ways; Walter, James and Jane's youngest son, was killed in action, and also the outlying shops closed never to open again. After the war it was decided to open a shop in central London, and Ogden's became a limited company. J R O went to the capital, disguised himself as a working man, and walked the streets of St. James watching where the wealthy did their shopping. Eventually he found suitable premises in Duke Street, opposite Mason's Yard, and obtained a lease. He placed this new branch under the direction of his three sons, each working in London on a weekly rota system, returning to Harrogate at weekends. The sons made a great success of the enterprise, and in 1925 William left the company and opened his own business in London.

*Above, Ogden's solid silver model of
the Harrogate Royal Pump Room;
below, a 1937 advertisement from
The Illustrated London News,
pronouncing Ogden's involvement
with the Coronation of King
George*

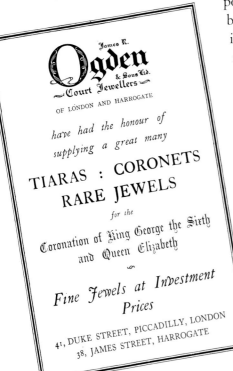

As the sons took a greater charge of the business J R O gave more time to his interest in archaeology and following the discovery of the tomb of King Tutankhamun he developed a slide show so that others might share in his knowledge. In 1931 the Daily Express recorded that James' lectures had already raised over £40,000 for charity. During all this activity the Ogden shops reflected the current trends and responded to customers' wishes for items that were fashionable, well designed and of excellent quality.

Ogden's most famous beautiful creation from their workshops was a solid silver model of the Harrogate Royal Pump Room ordered by Captain Whitworth, who was Mayor of Harrogate in 1926-27-28, and who gave the model to the town. It was in 1928 that Ogdens acquired the adjoining shop, 40 James Street, this giving them much larger premises, especially important being the added window space for their spectacular displays.

The Coronation of King George VI brought much business to the company. Many fine pieces of jewellery were bought by Ogdens and then resold to distinguished customers; in other instances clients brought in family heirlooms for conversion into contemporary items.

When the Second World War began J R Ogden started to dispose of the various specialist collections he had built up of books, newspaper cuttings, antiquities and photographs, many items going to specialist libraries, but much of the local material staying in the town. Having completed the task he died on the 13 April 1940; the Harrogate Council, of which he had been a member, stood in silent respect. His obituary was long and glowing, as deserved by a man of his stature; it did not dwell on his business achievements but on the quality of the man, 'He went about doing good'. During the War Jack Ogden was killed by a bomb in London, but the firm carried on, although several members of the family were on active service. In the 1950s the company made a splendid civic mace for presentation to the city of Wellington, in New Zealand. James Robert Ogden II became chairman of the company in 1940 and on his death in 1969 Jack's son Denis became managing director. In 1982 Glen Ogden, Denis's elder son, became managing director. No 40 James Street has been relinquished, but No 38 is still an institution in the world of fine jewellery, silver and precious stones, still retaining a great deal of its Edwardian atmosphere.

E. OLDROYD & SONS (LOFTHOUSE) LTD.

John Oldroyd was a well-known figure in the Friday Bridge area of Wisbech. He grew top fruit, strawberries, and was a prominent pig dealer. It was not unusual for his sons to herd hundreds of pigs from the station, along country lanes, to the farm. However in the depression he lost everything, including his land, and decided to move to Yorkshire, near to his daughter, Martha Neal, who had a greengrocer's shop in Northgate, Wakefield. He rented Pymont Farm at Lofthouse, near Wakefield.

Martha continually complained to her father that she could not purchase high quality fruit and vegetables locally and eventually persuaded him to once again use his considerable expertise in growing such produce. So great was the demand for this that he sent for his eldest son, Ernest, Ernest's wife and their young son John Kenneth (Ken) to come and assist him on the farm. John became friendly with one of the local rhubarb growers and taught him about growing strawberries – in exchange he told John some of the secrets of forcing rhubarb. Not having a

forcing shed John converted a barn for the purpose, growing rhubarb on the ground floor but placing another floor above it on which he reared chickens. John took great delight in passing on his new found knowledge to young Ken so that he also could achieve the very best from the rhubarb roots.

Ernest was more interested in growing strawberries and vegetables than rhubarb and he had a pony and cart with which he started a greengrocery round; this later expanded into several rounds supplying fruit and vegetables direct to the public. John eventually returned to Friday Bridge, Wisbech where he died, but Ernest stayed on and bought Pymont Farm.

Due to Ernest's poor health his son Ken took over the business at an early age and was keen to develop the farm into a much bigger enterprise, eventually taking over farms in Carlton and Rothwell. Today he is joined in the business, which now covers over 300 acres in Carlton village and surrounding area, by his son John Graham, daughter Janet and son-in-law Neil; about 100 acres of the farm is given over to rhubarb production.

Rhubarb first came to this country from Siberia in the 16th century, but it wasn't until the 18th century that its culinary qualities were discovered, although in other parts of the world there are records of its roots having been used as a drug in 2700BC.

It is believed that the forcing of rhubarb first happened by accident in Chelsea in 1817. The growing of forced rhubarb in Yorkshire dates from 1877, and subsequently it declined everywhere else, mainly due to the conditions the crop requires. There were, however, other reasons why rhubarb forcing has been such a major success in the

Ernest Oldroyd's rhubarb first won the British Championship in 1968

area between Leeds and Wakefield. One would seem to be the plants' affinity with the local soil, another the close proximity of the Yorkshire coal-field, and also the extensive rail network of 100 years ago. Local industries had a real contribution to make, for not only was there cheap local coal but also 'shoddy', a waste product from the woollen industry, which was used as a slow release nitrogenous organic fertilizer.

At one time rhubarb growers could be counted in their hundreds in this area but there are now only about 18 and of these only three are major suppliers. Over the winter months Oldroyds produce 100-150 tons of forced rhubarb, and this supplies both London and Scottish markets, in addition to 'green' rhubarb (field grown rhubarb) which is often used to bulk up other fruits in jams, to flavour yoghurt, and even in the base of coned ice creams.

Rhubarb roots are planted in the fields surrounding the home base for two to three years, to build up the root,

Above, rhubarb is forced in sheds and right, packed on site

before they are lifted to go into the forcing sheds. During these formative years no rhubarb is 'pulled', all the goodness being allowed to return to the rootstock each autumn. In the year when the roots are to be lifted the Oldroyds note the first frost and then count the accumulative 'units' of frost, at six inches below soil level, until a certain level is reached, this varying from variety to variety. Only when the roots have received the required units of frost can they be successfully forced. The roots must be carefully lifted from the fields, ensuring that the dormant buds are not damaged, and then they are placed tightly together in the dark sheds. A thin covering of soil is laid over the roots and this is then watered in so that the crowns are absolutely free of soil or grit which might scratch the delicate young growths. To prevent the rhubarb leaves turning green even the picking is carried out by candle-light! The rhubarb is then graded before being carefully packed in lined boxes for transportation to the wholesale market.

In 1995 Ken Oldroyd had conferred upon him the Northern Horticultural Society's highest award, the Harlow Carr Medal, in recognition of his outstanding work on the commercial growing of rhubarb and vegetables.

Each year the National Rhubarb Championships are held in the area in early February, a tradition which began almost 80 years ago, when local growers compete against each other. The grower with the most points gained from a range of classes is judged Champion for the year! Ken, now 72, still enjoys nothing better than caring for the family's award winning strains of rhubarb, developed over four generations, and which when forced, and stewed, give so much delight to many.

W.R. OUTHWAITE & SON
Ropemakers

Rope making has been carried on in the dales for well over 250 years. In the Askrigg parish records Joseph Brenkley of Setbusk [Sedbusk, near Hawes] was described as a rope-maker at the time of his death in 1725.

In the census returns for Hawes in 1841 Thomas Wharton, and his sons, Richard and John, are listed as ropemakers. By 1851 they also employed an apprentice, 13-year-old William Simpson, as a wheelturner; it was his job to turn the wheel that put the twist into the rope. They made the ropes at the Old Toll Bar, later known as the Gate House, on the road leading to Ingleton, and as the ropewalk ran parallel to the toll-road passers-by would be able to watch the family at work.

In 1905 Johnny 'Roper' Wharton, grandson of the founder, sold the business, 'retiring' at the age of 38, having spent at least 24 years making rope. The business was taken over by William Richard Alfred 'Billy Dick' Outhwaite, who had previously worked for the Whartons, but whose family had been farmers at Raydaleside for generations. Now Billy Dick moved to Hawes and became a full-time rope maker. To begin with he continued to make ropes at Gate House, selling most of these at Hawes market. Even though the railway had come to Hawes, Billy Dick still travelled the long exposed road to Kettlewell once a year by pony and cart with a load of ropes.

W R Outhwaite threading a loom for weaving webbing in the early 1940s

Billy Dick and his wife had a son Thomas Gardner Outhwaite, in 1911. He became the second generation of the Outhwaite ropemakers. In 1922 Mr. Outhwaite had to leave Gate House and he managed to acquire Banker's Field at Town Foot, which was on the route between the auction mart and the railway station.

Frequently farmers and locals congregated in the ropemaking shed to discuss politics, religion and village gossip – both adults and children enjoyed the company of Mr. Outhwaite, and willingly they turned the handle for him whilst he made the ropes.

During the Second World War the Ministry of Supply controlled the allocation of hemp, coir and jute used in rope-making.. After the war Tom, Billy Dick's son, joined his father in the business and the firm became W R Outhwaite & Son. In 1952 Tom got a grant from the Yorkshire Rural Industries Council to install an electric motor to power the twisting machine. Mr Outhwaite Snr continued to take an active interest in the business until shortly before his death in 1956, aged 81.

Tom Outhwaite soon discovered how lonely a job it could be working on your own. In 1961 he displayed his work at the Great Yorkshire Show, taking with him 12 dozen cow halters, intending to sell them at 4s 6d each. He returned home having sold them at £1 each, and with orders for many more!

As Tom came near to retiring, and with no obvious successor, ropemaking in Hawes appeared to be doomed, but as he described the

T G Outhwaite creates the first twist for a clothes line

situation to two visitors to Hawes in 1974, new hope was born. Peter and Ruth Annison were college lecturers in Nottingham; they had no knowledge of running a business and knew nothing of ropemaking! However they both knew the area intimately and felt sure that Peter's experience as a textile chemist would be valuable. They took over the business in July 1975, 'overlapping' Tom Outhwaite for four months until his retirement.

Soon the Annisons were making multi-coloured skipping ropes and macrame plant pot holders to meet the tourist demand, in addition to the various agricultural ropes, but it wasn't until 1976 that they felt they could afford to take on a full-time member of staff, Norman Chapman. In 1978 they introduced a mail order service. After small extensions in 1977, in 1980 they built a longer indoor ropewalk and also replaced Mr Outhwaite's wooden building which had given such good service over the past 50 and more years.

Today the premises have been further extended and the range of items produced is much wider. Although agricultural ropes are still made they are no longer a major part of the business, and bell ropes for churches are now a speciality. It is still possible to see the traditional materials, sisal, flax, jute and cotton, with the exception of hemp, being used alongside man-made fibres such as polypropylene yarn. Innovative techniques have been developed by the Annisons, for instance in the production of wicks for candles, where the wick has to be specially treated with various chemicals to make it burn properly, before being dried and then wound onto reels and sold to candle-makers. Plaited cords for light-pulls, carrier-bag handles and anorak draw-cords are among the many items made at Hawes, whilst fine twines can be seen alongside the heavier ropes used for bannisters and for crowd barriers.

At the turn of the century, products from Outhwaite's probably went no further than the lower dales, but today they are exported to over 20 countries. Peter and Ruth Annison ensure that traditional items can still be obtained, made in time-honoured ways, but additionally they and their staff have developed new products and new techniques to make ropemaking an economic success in 20th century Britain. Looking ahead to the 21st century new ideas are being developed to build on the heritage of the past.

Rope-making today at the Wensleydale factory

PLAXTON
Coach & Bus

Frederick William Plaxton opened a joinery workshop in Bar Street, Scarborough, in 1907. Prior to the First World War the firm had become a building contractor and had won important contracts for the Town Hall, the Futurist Cinema, the Cumberland Hotel, and the Girls' High School.

During the First World War he took over the Olympia Skating Rink and made shell boxes and wooden aircraft parts; it could be said this was his first venture into the world of transport! Also in 1917 a young Tom Stephenson joined the company as a junior clerk; he was to stay with them for the next fifty years, eventually becoming joint managing director.

After the war there was an element of 'swords into ploughshares' and Plaxtons offered expertise and facilities for making timber-framed car bodies, some of these cars being used by members of the royal family. The first Plaxton 'charabanc' body was built onto a Model T Ford chassis.

The first Plaxton works designed for the manufacture of vehicle bodies was Castle Works, named because they looked out onto Castle Road, which led up to Scarborough Castle – the Castle became the company's symbol and was used on letterheads and company papers.

The volume and reputation of Plaxton bodywork grew sharply with up to five bodies being turned out each week, generally on Crossley chassis; such Crossley cars were ordered for the Royal family, especially for overseas tours. Indeed Plaxton built a fleet of saloon bodies for Crossley cars for the Prince of Wales' tour of Australia in 1922, and this order was followed by others for royal cars for use in other parts of the world, as well as for a Crossley special limousine body for a car for King George V.

As time passed Plaxton became involved in making bodies for Sunbeam and Daimler chassis and later set up a subsidiary company to build Weymann 'flexible' bodywork, under licence, for Hillman and Lagonda chassis. The Weymann design of fabric covered bodies used a system of metal brackets to eliminate squeaks and rattles, avoiding contact between the various

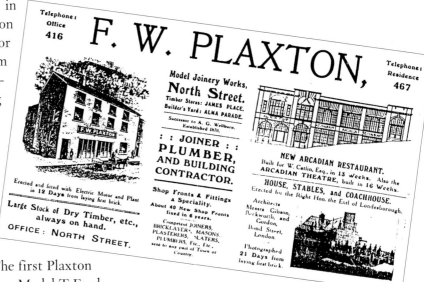

wooden components of the body frame. Gradually the making of car-bodies declined, especially during the depression years, but a repair and renovation service was offered until the start of the Second World War.

The first customer for a Plaxton 'coach' was Edgar Helston Robinson, a Scarborough bus proprietor. Charabanc body production in those early days tended to be a localised trade, and Plaxton was one of several coach building companies who began their days in a seaside resort but later attained national status.

E H Robinson's operated charabancs from the station yard and a bus service operated by agreement with the local tramways company, Scarborough and District Motor Services, this later being taken over by United Automobile Services. Robinson was for several years a regular Plaxton customer, and it is possible that some of his purchases were for selling to other operators, not least because the last order he placed was for 23 convertible bodies on Lancia Pentiota chassis, although he only operated

The old and the new... above a 1963 Consort IV Bedford J2S, and right, a 1995 Excaliber on a Dennis chassis

about eleven Lancias in his own fleet. These charabancs were mainly 23 seater vehicles, forerunners of the centre-gangway coaches which often had an opening canvas roof.

Even though it was still a small business the second prize in the section for single-deck buses in the commercial bodywork competition at the 1931 Olympia Show was awarded to 'Messrs F W Plaxton'; indeed in 1936 Mr Plaxton was still running the business as a private venture, which probably explains why they are not mentioned

in the Motor Transport Year Book – there was no registered company of that name.

In 1936 a large new works was built in Seamer Road, which was extended almost immediately to cater for an increased rate of production. Soon Plaxton bodied coaches were becoming a familiar sight over much of northern England. As such reliable chassis as the Leyland Tiger and AEC's Regal and Reliance became available it became common practice for operators, after they had had their coaches for six to eight years, to send them to firms such as Plaxtons for rebodying. Coach bodies developed distinctive styles, not least those of Plaxtons, although some operators still wanted vehicles to satisfy their own ideas. In 1937 Frederick William Plaxton jnr. joined the company at the age of eighteen. To avoid confusion his name was cropped to Eric; his sister Gladys also became a director.

During the Second World War the Seamer Road works was turned into a munitions factory. In 1943 a fire caused serious damage to the works.

With the war over, 1946 saw the resumption of bodybuilding, and wooden-framed coach bodies were fitted to Bedford, Commer, Austin, Leyland and AEC chassis. The bodies had gently-curved styling in the spirit of the period and there was an unprecedented demand. Plaxtons became recognised as a national company, now supplying such major names as Wallace Arnold and Charles Rickards, Royal Warrant Holders for coach hire. In the 1950s the company diversified, producing a fire engine body for the North Riding of Yorkshire County Council and later over 400 Ministry of Works Fire Tenders (better known as the Green Goddesses) as well as over 70 mobile canteens for the United States Air Force.

It became common for the body design to include the front of the vehicles as engines were fitted under the floor, instead of at the front. Other innovations included the driver sitting in the passenger compartment, improved heating and demisting, and bigger bodies with larger seating capacities. From 1954 the link between the Bedford SB and Plaxton became more common, a combination previously linked only with Duple bodyworks. In the first British Coach Rally held in 1955 Plaxton-bodied entries were only 4.5% but by 1958 this had risen to 21%, only outnumbered by Duple. The Plaxton Venturer was one of the first to fit curved glass corner sections to the front windscreen. The company also moved into large scale bus-body building using traditional timber framed construction.

F W Plaxton died in 1957 and Eric succeeded him as chairman. The following year British coach operators were offered the Plaxton Panorama, a coach with long side-windows and forced-air ventilation; it was a major step forward in coach design. In 1961 a major new works was established at Eastfield on a 45 acre site.

Another great achievement was in 1962 when Plaxton was the largest exhibitor in the British Coach Rally. Both the overall winner and the concours winner, in which marks are allotted for appearance, were Plaxton Panorama coaches, although the bulk of the entries were Plaxton Embassy coaches.

In 1961 Plaxton became a public limited company and entered the export market. As the motorway network expanded long distance travel also grew and operators sacrificed carrying capacity to ensure passengers had the comfort of improved leg-room and reclining seats. By 1967 the number of bodybuilders had fallen to only two, Plaxton and Duple. In 1968 the Plaxton Elite was introduced, with large curved-glass side-windows. Plaxton had become the largest builder of public service vehicles (buses and coaches) in the country, producing over 1000 units per year, growing to 1300 in 1973. By 1978 the factory had switched entirely to steel framed construction. Following the continental trend, high-floored coaches were introduced in 1977 – Plaxton created the Viewmaster body. For the 1979 season a small coach was introduced using the Bedford CF light van chassis, providing seating for 17 passengers.

The early 1980s and 1990s have shown a continued trend for luxury coaches, with tables, toilets, televisions and air-conditioning. The trend in bus design has been towards midi- and minibus and the company are market leaders in these

areas, the Beaver being the best selling minibus with over 2,000 now in use throughout Britain.

1995 saw the Henlys Group, who now own Plaxton, acquire Northern Counties of Wigan, an old established bus body builder well-known for its double-deck buses. In 1996 Plaxton pioneered the articulated coach in Britain, built on a Volvo chassis, and are currently involved in research into the uses of buses powered by LPG (liquified petroleum gas) and CNG (compressed natural gas).

Plaxton is today part of Henlys group plc, one of Britain's biggest motor trade groups, with a £390 million turnover in 1994. F W (Eric) Plaxton died in 1995 at the age of 75, leaving much of his money for the benefit of the people of Scarborough.

The main Ponden Mill was built near the end of the 18th century by Robert Heaton, of Ponden House, who was the owner of a considerable number of properties in the Haworth and Keighley area, but an even earlier mill dates back to the early 18th century and was used for milling corn. Robert Heaton's mill was originally built to spin cotton yarns but from 1898 until 1973 it was used by Robert Sunderland & Son to produce worsted materials. Until the late 1930s the mill was powered by a water wheel, supplemented by a steam engine, when there was no water.

Barry Brookfield grew up with cotton, for it was in the air he breathed in Bolton. In the 1930s and '40s Bolton was very much a mill town and his parents lived in a terrace house, with a mill at either end of the street. His father was a self employed upholsterer, but there was very little money to spare and life was not easy.

When Barry left school he went to the Bolton Art School for a year. He had a great interest in shops and window design and would spend hours looking around the town, but his real love was the local market. Here he would talk with the stall holders, would get them to let him help, earning a few shillings to help out at home. He loved to hear the 'pitching', the market men and women shouting their phrases, to draw the passers-by, turning them into potential customers.

His first full-time job was as a shop junior at the Co-op in Bolton. They didn't trust him to serve; Barry's main job seemed to be sweeping the pavement outside the store! But he did want to learn about selling and soon he got a job at Saxone. In a busy shoe shop he learned that it was important not only to sell shoes but also to get the customer to have socks and polish. Barry learned much in that shop and many of the training methods he experienced there he still uses in his business today. However shop pay was low and he needed more money; he also must work in the mill!

In the mill Barry learnt about warp and weft and all the other technical terms used in the cloth trade. Little did he realise what a useful background this would be in years to come. But there were to be other jobs before he could put his knowledge of textiles into action; for three years he was a RAF Police Dog Handler, then sold shop fittings, before he took a job selling toiletries for a manufacturing chemist. He sold the toiletries to market traders and was amazed at the quantities the stall holders were able to 'move'.

At that time Barry had little capital; two weeks pay and £70 holiday money, but he had the germ of an idea – he too would become a market trader! He kept his job with the chemist but on a Saturday he had a stall on Leigh market selling towel seconds. The cotton mill would only sell him bits but these he bundled up and

Ponden Mill, built in the late 18th century

sold by weight. He now willingly admits that he was very 'green'.

Barry was very determined, very hungry for success but he found it was difficult to get a pitch on the markets. The bank would not give him credit and so he had to buy on a daily basis. He chose tea towels as his main line, realising they would give a quick turnover and learnt his business from his customers, for they knew textiles better than he did. He quickly realised that he must know what the housewives wanted to buy, and the goods had to be at a price they wanted to pay! Quality was most important – if he satisfied their wants he believed he would have a customer for life. He listened to the customers, he had great rapport with people and he struggled to find the right supplies for each particular market. The mills always had surpluses, but he had to ensure that what he bought was good quality.

On one occasion, having looked at the Markets Yearbook, he went to the free street market in Kendal. He arrived to find there was no market and that the nearest was at Barrow, a non-textile town. He arrived at lunchtime, put a tarpaulin on the ground and piled it with towels, blankets and sheets. He had been up since 5am and promptly fell asleep but was quickly awakened to find people around him – customers!

On another occasion he was told he would make his fortune at Bakewell Bank Holiday Fair. He spent his every penny on stock but found the market full of experienced pitchers shouting to attract customers. Barry's spot, however, was down a quiet alley in a small pig pen with very few customers. Later in the afternoon, with an almost empty till, disaster struck. A torrential downpour flooded the market and Barry's stock; he faced ruin. After a sleepless night he went to Rochdale market and using Dayglo poster pens announced 'Flood Damaged Stock'. Remembering the pitchers at Bakewell he jumped on the stall, forgot his shyness and began pitching 'they may be wringing wet, but they're cheap'. He soon sold out, and he had his best trading day ever. The lesson learnt – tell the customers why it's a bargain and use a bit of theatre.

Barry is a great observer, always trading with an 'open door' – never having it shut; he realised the importance of creating activity, rapport. At the front of the stall he had 'pick up lines' – dusters, dish cloths, etc., ones to entice the customer. Eventually he settled in Skipton and became very well known. Whilst there he went to an exhibition in London and saw, for the first time, duvets

Above, Barry Brookfield; below, Ponden Mill as advertised in 1976

and nylon sheets. They were innovations and retailers had been slow to pick them up. They were to be a line he would become famous for.

Gradually he outgrew his market stalls. They provided a good income but they did not stimulate him any more; being in a shop did not appeal either. By this time he was living in a farmhouse in Grassington which had a barn attached. He decided to keep his stock in the barn, but there were mites in the barn, they got into the stock and it all had to be burnt. He

One of Ponden Mill's 30 outlets

needed a proper warehouse, he could not bear just to store stuff.

In February 1973 the country was in a state of complete upheaval. Workers were on a three day week, but Barry had just taken Ashmount Mills in Haworth and he had to open! He hung his advertising on the back of the Brontë country: 'Come to Haworth – don't freeze at home. Learn about continental quilts!' He had done his research and he opened his Duvet centre. He brought the duvets in from Austria, but as he could not get duvet covers he converted sheets and other fabric and made covers himself. It was

instantly successful, but he hadn't secured a lease on the property and he was served notice to quit! He had only been trading six months; now he had six months notice to go.

The only place he could find was a derelict mill in the middle of nowhere. It had no car parking, no planning permission for retail sales, and the vendors were asking £30,000 – it was virtually unsaleable! Barry Brookfield bought Ponden Mill for £15,000. It was about three miles from Haworth on the narrow moor road to Colne.

Still he had difficulties with the planners and applications were turned down. When McLintock, who made quilts at Northallerton, went into liquidation, he bought their quilt filling machine and installed it at Ponden Mill. He eventually opened to the public but then had to persuade people to come – he encouraged Women's Institutes and other similar bodies to come and see hand weaving, clogs being made, see a potter at the wheel, and even have a cup of tea, as well as buy his goods. He put in his own licensed restaurant and opened on Sundays; Ponden had become a tourist attraction!

The fame of Ponden Mill grew on the sale of duvets. He offered £5 for old clean blankets, to encourage people to buy duvets, and gave the blankets to the Red Cross and other good deserving causes.

Such a development as Ponden Mill proved hard to repeat successfully but in 1985 Barry Brookfield opened Darley Mill, in Nidderdale, a few miles from Harrogate. Subsequently he has developed town centre shops, at first in secondary locations, but latterly in prime sites. Today there are 30 Ponden Mill outlets, all selling a wide range of goods, but with textiles as the core items, and gradually a nationwide framework will be developed.

CHRISTOPHER
PRATTS

Gunnerside in Swaledale, way up in the Yorkshire Dales, must have been an isolated hamlet in 1819 when Christopher Pratt was born there at Bents House to William and Annas, the ninth of their thirteen children. With such a large family William needed to augment his income as a smallholder and he worked at 'Old Gang' lead mine, about three miles up Gunnerside Gill. In winter the family knitted stockings to earn a little extra money; no doubt Christopher helped as well by taking food to the mine for his father and older brothers.

In 1825 William died, leaving the family in desperate poverty. Annas' parents had kept the pub in Gunnerside, but moved to Bradford where her father built houses in George Street. Annas persuaded him to let her make a new home in one of these houses and the family made the 75-mile journey which took two days.

Joseph Nutter, a craftsman and cabinet maker, was having three houses, a showroom and a workshop built at 33 North Parade in thriving Bradford. Born in Halifax in 1799 he had been orphaned at an early age and at 13 had come to Bradford to be apprenticed to his brother, a cabinet maker in Darley Street. Joseph retired in 1850, but on his death in 1884 he left more than £20,000, including £10,000 for the founding of an orphanage.

Christopher Pratt was apprenticed to Joseph Nutter; he stayed with him until 1845 when he started his own business in Brummitts Yard off Darley Street. In 1842 Christopher married Jane Cheesbrough who, unlike Christopher, had had 'proper schooling', and was not without money. As a young girl of 14 she had left the family home in Snape, near Bedale, and come to keep house for her brothers in Bradford

Christopher must have become well known in Bradford, for on the day he started on his own, two wealthy people offered to help him, one with an order, the other willing to stand surety at the bank for up to £500. Christopher soon moved his workshop to behind the County Court on Manor Row. When Joseph Nutter retired Christopher Pratt was joined by Thomas Prince, and together they took over Joseph's stock, plant and lease at 33 North Parade, trading as Pratt & Prince. Thomas Prince was an elderly man who had worked for

Annas Pratt mother of the founder Christopher (right); below, the North Parade, Bradford, premises last century

87

An early billhead showing the range of services

Joseph Nutter as a woodcarver. He also had money, and to Christopher that was important.

Christopher and Jane Pratt moved to live at North Parade and the ever-energetic Jane was capable of turning her hand to anything in the business. She took charge of the sewing room and supervised the planning and making-up of furnishing draperies, all carried out in one of their bedrooms. In 1854 the family moved to Cemetery Cottage, near Undercliffe Cemetery.

Christopher always preferred to dine at home and at mid-day he would hire a cab, which waited for 20 minutes at the cemetery gates, while he ate his meal; then it was back to the shop, as salesman or with his coat off, planning and cutting carpets for fitting. His evenings were spent either with bookwork or making furniture for orders. Three years later the Pratts and their eight children moved to Moorside at Eccleshill, where they lived until they had Highcliffe House built on Eccleshill Moor.

After 1840 the standard of living improved, good furniture was in demand and the firm prospered. By the turn of the century Pratts had 14 departments capable of providing a complete house furnishing and decorating service. From the mid-19th century Pratt & Prince were buying ready-made furniture from leading London wholesalers and provincial manufacturers. They also designed furniture themselves, and many of the sketches, some in colour, are still in existence; this allowed individual customers to commission furniture. To complete the home furnishings, patterns were produced for wallpapers, fabrics and ornamental friezes. Some furniture was even produced 'bespoke', chairs were made to fit the customer.

In 1892 Christopher and Jane celebrated their Golden Wedding. A photograph taken then shows the 43 descendants of the family; there had been no deaths. Christopher was a town councillor twice, a leading Free Mason, and closely associated with the Wesleyan Methodists – through Eastbrook Chapel, and also in the wider circuit. In 1893 the couple went to live at Holly Hill at Well near Bedale.

The firm were pioneers in the making and fitting of individual tip-up seats in public halls; for many years they also made the Bradford Desk, a registered design described as "A Dumb Home Secretary – accessible at all times, yet instantly private at will, always attendant with ink, paper and pen, it stops

The cabinet workshops in 1908

procrastination and guards unfinished work until wanted again".

In 1874 Prince retired and in 1880 a partnership was formed between Christopher and his sons William, Thomas and Job Cheesbrough, the name being changed to Christopher Pratt & Sons. Shortly after this Pratts became agents for Liberty & Co. of London, and allocated a department to their merchandise, but the exotic designs were not to the taste of Pratts' customers who were mainly conservative middle class.

By 1903, on his father's death, Thomas Pratt was in sole control of the business and was joined by his two eldest sons, Leonard and Christopher. Christopher jnr became a notable designer; three younger brothers joined them in subsequent years.

Bradford's wool barons moved out to the surrounding towns of Harrogate, Ilkley and even Morecambe, but they still patronised Pratts. Other work came from equipping banks, town halls, churches and in 1902 they won a contract for over £9,000 to furnish the new Scalebor Park Asylum at Burley in Wharfedale. Other commissions followed, including furnishing the County Hall at Wakefield, and Morley and Dewsbury town halls.

In 1925 a radio department was opened with a radio repair shop and an accumulator charging plant, for many homes had no electricity and dry batteries were still uncommon. During the Second World War, Pratts made boxes for machine-gun parts and bunks for air-raid shelters. They were designated to manufacture utility furniture, only available to those who were bombed-out or newly weds setting up their first home – on 'units' (furniture was also rationed!)

A 1920s wireless set at Pratts; left, an advertisement from the 1927 Wesleyan Methodist Conference handbook on its visit to Bradford

A fourth generation of the Pratt family joined the business in 1940 and 1950, followed by three members of the fifth generation in more recent years. Sentiment has decreed that the original corner premises erected by Joseph Nutter in 1839 would not be dismantled and this explains the variation in floor levels in the present shop.

After trading as a family business for 150 years, the retail home furnishing division changed hands, another family business became the new owners of 33 North Parade. The name, staff and traditions of quality, value and personal service continue as before.

The interior design and manufacturing division now trades as Christopher Pratts Contracts Ltd from premises at Cheapside, with a works unit at Brick Lane Mills, Bradford. Serving the needs of commerce, it provides specialist joinery for offices and shops, banks and building societies.

A 5th generation member of the Pratt family, Christopher Pratt, is now involved in this enterprise.

RECKITT & COLMAN

When somebody suggested to Isaac Reckitt in the late 1830s that he go into starch production he little knew what he was starting. Isaac's great-great grandfather, Thomas, farmed near Gainsborough in the 17th century, coming under the influence of George Fox, founder of the Quakers, and down the centuries the Reckitts have been connected with the Quakers. Isaac was no exception.

He and his brother, Thomas, were involved in corn milling (they built the five-sailed Maud Foster mill on the outskirts of Boston which is still in working order) but times were hard and Isaac withdrew from the partnership.

Another corn venture in Nottingham did not prosper and Isaac and his wife Ann moved to Hull where they had friends and relatives. One friend was particularly helpful with the 'starch suggestion'. On 1st October 1840, after closing his Nottingham business, Isaac started up at the Starch Works in Hull – and an epic was born. Isaac's brother, John, stood surety for the £150 annual rent, and £621 paid for existing stock and packing materials was part of a loan from friends and relatives.

For the first nine years he only produced starch, from wheat flour to which smalt, a blue pigment, was added for whitening. Early sales were in the Hull district, mainly through agents, as they had no travellers. One year when the works were flooded their 14 year old son Francis came home from Ackworth School to work a pump, thereby saving a labourer's wage.

Isaac and Ann lived in St. Quintin's Place but in 1849 moved to Williamson Street, where they lived for the rest of their lives. Their eldest son Charles died of consumption in 1842, and the following year 18 year old George returned to the family business to 'go on the road', again saving a salary as well as agent charges. To increase income Isaac kept pigs which he fed on by-products from the starch works and also became a share-broker, but this was not profitable. A breakthrough came in 1844 when the firm started to sell Soluble Starch and George extended the areas he covered from Newcastle to London.

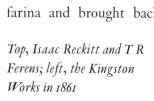

In 1846 Isaac Reckitt went to Lille to find a new source of farina and brought back sago

Top, Isaac Reckitt and T R Ferens; left, the Kingston Works in 1861

flour. It is said that Isaac received a formula for making starch from sago in settlement of a bad debt.

There was great concern when the Reckitts heard that their works were to be sold but the negotiations dragged on and by 1848 they were able to afford to buy them for £1125. That year George was made a partner and the firm became Isaac Reckitt & Son. Gradually the company prospered, but there was intense competition from both Brown & Polson, and Colmans.

As trade grew they had to find ways of increasing production and started packing by machinery. Younger brothers Francis and James joined George on the road, travelling in open third-class railway carriages or by coach, and staying overnight at temperance hotels which were cheaper and quieter.

The younger generation pressed their father to start advertising as they were working from 5.30am until 9pm, then catching a train after that, and still not managing to see everybody. Showcards were designed for customers to display, some of these were enclosed in gilt frames covered by plate glass; handbills were also printed for house to house distribution. In 1851 they took part in the Great Exhibition.

1852 saw the introduction of several new lines, including Laundry Blue and Black-Lead. By 1858 Isaac had paid off all the original loans, but at 66 his hard life was taking effect and he died four years later. The business was shared equally by brothers George, Francis and James, who became partners. Export orders for their products were increasing, including ones from Canada and New Zealand, and now they installed a plant for making starch from rice.

T R Ferens was not quite 21 when he was appointed confidential and shorthand secretary to James Reckitt, in 1868, at £70 a year. At 26 he was appointed works manager of the Blue and Black-Lead mills, the sawmill and the packing room; he also became responsible for laboratory tests.

In 1879 Reckitt & Sons Ltd was formed, all the shares being held by the company, and Francis was appointed the first chairman. James and George became directors and T R Ferens company secretary.

A labourer's pay in 1862 was 5d an hour for a 59 hour week. Paris Blue, introduced in 1873, was a great success and overseas sales remained good. In 1888 Mr Ferens became general manager when Francis Reckitt retired; by this time the expansion of the company was rapid and to provide extra capital Reckitts became a public company. In 1894 James was awarded a baronetcy, for services to the Liberal Party and the community.

Just before the turn of the century Reckitts introduced Robin Starch, but in Lancashire and

Yorkshire Dolly Blue was the popular competing brand. To counter this Reckitts introduced Bag Blue, whilst in the south Paris Blue continued to be successful.

In Australia liquid metal polishes were used and Reckitts introduced Brasso in 1905 and Silvo in 1912. A year later they formed the Chiswick Polish Co., with the Mason brothers, who brought with them Cherry Blossom and Mansion Polish. Reckitts were also offered Persil by Henkel of Dusseldorf, but they declined and it was taken up by Lever Brothers.

In 1907 Sir James Reckitt wrote to Ferens: "Whilst I and my family live in beautiful houses, surrounded by lovely gardens and fine scenery, the workpeople we employ are, many of them, living in squalor, and all of them without

gardens in narrow streets and alleys. It seems the time has come, either alone, or in conjunction with some members of the Board, to establish a Garden Village, within a reasonable distance of our Works, so that those who are wishful might have the opportunity of living in a better house, with a garden, for the same rent that they now pay for a house in Hull – with the advantages of fresher air. ...As I am prepared, if necessary, to subscribe £100,000 the project will no doubt go on, ..." The Garden Village was officially opened in 1908, consisting of over 600 houses and other amenities.

1921 saw the introduction of Zebo liquid grate polish; Fast Dyes, Bath Cubes, and Windolene soon followed, then Karpol, and with the purchase of the Harpic Company, the famous lavatory cleanser. Arthur Reckitt, Isaac's grandson, became joint chairman with T R Ferens, who had joined the company years earlier as the confidential and shorthand secretary! Ferens also served Hull as MP from 1906, for 13 years, and when he died in 1930 his fellow directors recorded their appreciation of all he had been and done.

In 1930 the company decided to concentrate on antiseptics and in 1933 introduced Dettol; 1937 they bought Steradent Denture Cleaner.

1938 was momentous: amalgamation with J & J Colman took place to form Reckitt & Colman Ltd, when Reckitts received about two-thirds of the share capital; it was the climax of negotiations started in 1909!

William Wren produced the first wax polish in 1884 in Northampton. It remained a family concern until 1938 when it was acquired by Chiswick Products; they merged with Reckitt & Colman in 1954. Over succeeding decades such products as Disprin, Steradent, Cherry Blossom, Mansion Polish, Cardinal Tile Polish, and many others have continued to be household names and carried the company forward.

In the early 1990s, the company recognised that it must focus on its strengths: a global portfolio of leading household products and over-the-counter pharmaceutical brands sold over a wide geographic base. It also decided to build a strong business in household products in the United States.One third of the company's business is now in the United States, one third in Europe, and one third in the rest of the world. Reckitt & Colman continues to be, or seeks to be, a market leader in the 120 countries it trades in around the world.

By 1930, Percy's parents had died and he became head of the household, living a bachelor existence with his oldest unmarried sister. He was now self-employed, laying tarmac drives and paths, and employing several men.

With the increase in motor vehicles the tram went into decline, not least because it operated in the middle of the road causing a hazard to other road users and passengers. As a result tram lines were removed but at night drivers had sub-consciously relied on the reflections of their head-lamps from the tramlines. Percy Shaw decided that this night time 'guide' must be substituted by some other reflecting device and the 'Cats Eye' was born.

One of the earlier forms had its reflectors pointing towards the heavens and could not reflect light from approaching vehicle headlamps. But the basic principles of the cast iron housing and the rubber

Percy Shaw was born at Lee Mount, Halifax, in 1890. When he was two years old the family moved to Boothtown Mansion, a large house dating back to 1769 – they needed a large house for Jimmy Shaw and his first wife Jane had three sons and four daughters; after Jane's death Jimmy and his second wife Esther Hannah had three daughters and four sons – all in sixteen-and-a-half years. Percy was from the second marriage.

Percy left school at thirteen and went to work in a blanket mill, carrying bobbins of wool from the winders to the weavers. He hated school but knew that if he wanted to get on he would have to study, so he took a commercial course at night school and then got a job as a book-keeper. Realising that chances of promotion were poor he then decided to learn a trade and went into engineering, serving an apprenticeship at a wire mill, making heald wires which were used in looms. Again he decided to move on as he was not earning enough to maintain the members of the family still at home..

Left, Percy Shaw after receiving his OBE in 1965; below, a short, heavy duty road stud

When Percy's father lost his job in a dye house which closed down, they formed a partnership undertaking odd jobs. In 1914, when war broke out, a carpet mill was contracted to make khaki puttees, but special heald wires were needed for the looms. Percy managed to win the contract for the supply of these wires; later they made cartridge cases and shell noses under government contract.

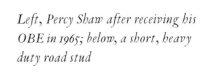

mounting pad containing the glass reflector units were to remain.

Soon after the company was incorporated in 1935 the 'Cats Eye' adopted its familiar shape with the rectangular rubber mounting holding the four reflective 'eyes', two either side of the pad, in a cast iron housing. The casting stood on four legs, its overall appearance resembling a neckless, tail-less cat which has eyes back and front – it is still the company's trademark!

Pre-war reflectors were of Czechoslovakian origin fitted tightly into sockets in the mould-ed rubber pad, and secured by small steel dowels. This early ver-sion was first installed at a halt line at the intersection of the Bradford-Wakefield road with the Leeds-Halifax road at Drighlington in

Above, Percy Shaw and his Rolls, checking studs above Halifax; right studs are installed by power drills

April 1935. They were quite effective for two or three weeks, until a spell of rain created mud on the road surface which got into the 'eyes', which then ceased to reflect. Since May 1935 all 'Cats Eyes' have incorporated a self-wiping cleaning device which is activated when the upper portion of the rubber mounting, containing the reflectors, is depressed by tyres of passing vehicles bringing the reflectors into contact with integral wipers in the rubber mounting.

Until 1939 all parts of the 'Cats Eye' were manufactured by other suppliers but since then the compo-nents have been manufactured 'in-house'. Over the years the design of the units has been modified to make them withstand increasing pressures and become more effective. A later problem was the increasing use of salt on icy roads, which had a bad effect on the reflective foil behind the sections of glass rod. This problem has been overcome by replacing the aluminium foil with a vacuum deposition of a film of pure aluminium directly onto the rear surface of the glass lens. This reflective film is then protected by several layers of high temperature bake epoxy paint which overlaps the 'aluminising' and adheres strongly to the glass. Further protection is provided by inserting the reflector into the rubber sleeve. The unit is then squeezed and sealed into the copper holder, preventing any corrosion.

The company employs about 130 staff and makes over one million roadstuds annually which are sold world-wide. Percy Shaw never moved from his home at Boothtown Mansion, adjacent to the former textile mill where 'Cats Eyes' are still made today. In 1965 he was awarded the OBE for his services to export; he died in 1976 but we will forever reflect on the life saving 'Cats Eyes' he gave us.

Nestlé

Mary Tuke, a Quaker who lived in York, opened a grocer's shop in the city in 1725. By 1785 this was run by her nephew and traded under the name of William Tuke & Sons; one of the products they sold was cocoa. In 1815 the firm described themselves as tea dealers, adding that they sold roasted coffee and manufactured chocolate.

In 1862 Henry Isaac Rowntree acquired the cocoa and chocolate side of the business which he quickly expanded. Henry's brother Joseph became his partner in 1869 and the company became H I Rowntree and Co. During the next ten years the company made 'Rock Cocoa', which was a blend of fine cocoa and sugar, and was sold in blocks; they also sold loose cocoa powder mixed with arrowroot or sago. They also made Chocolate Drops, Chocolate Creams, and penny and halfpenny cream balls.

Until 1879 fruit gums had been a monopoly of the French but they got Monsieur Gaget, a Frenchman, to take charge of this new department and in 1881 they also introduced Rowntree's Fruit Pastilles. To cope with the rapidly expanding trade they bought and converted a flour mill in 1882 and in 1890 bought the land, nearly 141 acres, where the present York factory stands. In 1897 the firm employed 1,200 workers, but by 1906 this had risen to 4,000!

In 1904 the Joseph Rowntree Village Trust was set up and in the next few years the company introduced schemes

Top, J Mackintosh, 1913; above, H Rowntree, 1870

to benefit their workers which included a widow's benefit fund, a workers' dining room and a gymnasium, and the appointment of an optician. They also gave workers an annual week's holiday with full pay and by 1919 reduced the working week to 44 hours.

Rowntree's Table Jellies were introduced in 1901 and in the 1930s several new lines were introduced, including the now popular Black Magic. To ensure the 'perfect chocolate assortment' 7,000 typical consumers were interviewed before Black Magic was developed. Other introductions of that decade were Kit Kat (then Chocolate Crisp) and Aero in 1935, Dairy Box in 1936, and Smarties in 1937. Polo was launched in 1948 and After Eight in 1962. Creamola Food Products and Sunpat Products Ltd became part of Rowntree's in 1966 and 1967.

John Mackintosh was born in Dukinfield, Cheshire, in 1868, the eldest surviving child of the eight children of Joseph and Mary Mackintosh. Joseph was a cotton spinner, and the family moved to Halifax a few months after John was born, so his father could take up a job as an overseer at Bowmans' new Halifax mill. When he was ten John started work as a 'half-timer', working six half days each week at Bowman Bros' mill; by the age of thirteen he was working full time, minding a pair of 'twiners' which twisted yarn into thread. In September 1890 John married Violet Taylor, but in April 1891 John's father died and from then on he also supported his widowed mother, five sisters, a brother who was training to be a minister, and his wife!

Shortly after setting up home in King

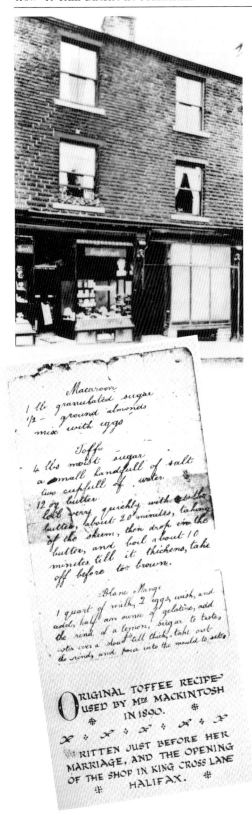

Macaroon
1 lb granulated sugar
1/2 - ground almonds
mix with eggs

Toffee
4 lbs moist sugar
a small handfull of salt
two cupfull of water.
12 oz butter
boil very quickly with butter
butter, about 20 minutes, taking
off the skum, then drop in the
butter, and boil about 10
minutes till it thickens, take
off before too brown.

Blanc Mange
1 quart of milk, 2 eggs wish and
add, half an ounce of gelatine, add
the rind of a lemon, sugar to tastes
stir over a slow till thick, take out
the rinds and pour into the mould to set

ORIGINAL TOFFEE RECIPE
USED BY Mrs MACKINTOSH
IN 1890.

WRITTEN JUST BEFORE HER
MARRIAGE, AND THE OPENING
OF THE SHOP IN KING CROSS LANE
HALIFAX.

Cross Street the couple decided to use their joint savings of £100 to open a pastry cook's shop where Violet did the baking and selling while John continued at the mill. However they soon felt they needed a speciality and decided it would be toffee. John had the idea of selling high quality toffee made from a combination of brittle English butterscotch and soft American caramel – they named it 'Mackintosh's Celebrated Toffee'.

John placed an advertisement inviting the public of Halifax to taste a free sample of the toffee, and long before closing time they were 'sold out'. Later he advertised again, "On Saturday last you were eating Mackintosh's toffee at our expense; next Saturday pay us another visit and eat it at your own expense". The result was overwhelming and very soon the sales of toffee far outstripped the monies from all the articles sold. People came to the 'Toffee Shop' from all over Halifax; gradually it became known throughout the country!

Within a year the upper floor of a tiny warehouse in nearby Hope Street was used for making the toffee, but in 1899 work commenced on a new factory in Queens Road, at a cost of £15,000. In 1909 the Queens Road factory was burnt down and the operation moved to an old factory, Albion Mills, which became the firm's permanent headquarters. Eventually the Queens Road factory was rebuilt and used for manufacturing chocolate and coating toffees.

John Mackintosh died in 1920; he had been an enlightened employer who developed good relationships with his staff, his suppliers and customers – all these stemming from his strong Christian faith. John and Violet had three children, Harold, Douglas and Eric, who all grew up in a home where the Sunday School had a big influence. They all entered the business and in 1921 John Mackintosh & Sons Ltd was formed.

Advertising was important to John and Harold and comic artists of the day, including Heath Robinson and Mabel Lucie Attwell, drew their ideas of Toffee Town for full page national newspaper advertisements. Their advertising policy was 'always quality first, publicity

Top, the King Cross shop in 1890; right, the original toffee recipe use d by Mrs Mackintosh in the same year

96

1935

1938

1952

1984

Above, Mackintosh's first pictorial advertisement; right, how the firm promoted fruit gums in 1955; left, the development of the Kit Kat

second, as advertising alone can only sell a poor article once!' Harold Mackintosh, later Lord Mackintosh, became a national figure through his work for the National Savings' movement.

1917 had seen the introduction of Toffee de Luxe but in 1936 their most famous selection was to make its debut – Quality Street. The name came from the play 'Quality Street' by J M Barrie, who also wrote 'Peter Pan'. The design was centred round the play's main characters, a soldier and his lady. At that time Quality Street sold at 6d a quarter pound and shopkeepers were urged to stock the new product with the slogan: 'Put your shop in Quality Street by putting Quality Street in your shop'. The United Kingdom assortment had seventeen different sweets, although the export assortment had to be varied slightly. Quality Street is still distinguished from its competitors by its wide variety of shapes, including fingers, squares, and triangles and by the bright designs of its wrappings. It is still exported to more than 100 countries, being particularly popular in Japan and the United States.

Other successful introductions have been Rolo in 1937, Good News in 1960 and Toffee Crisp and Tooty Fruities in 1963. In 1969 Rowntree and Mackintosh merged, and in 1988 Rowntree Mackintosh joined Swiss-owned Nestle SA becoming the Nestle Rowntree division of Nestle UK Ltd.

SEVEN SEAS

Cod liver oil has been used as a medicine for hundreds of years by the fishermen of Iceland, Greenland, Norway and Scotland but it was Dr. Kay, an eighteenth century physician at Manchester Infirmary, who first used it in the clinic. He gave doses of cod liver oil to people suffering from bone diseases and rheumatism, dispensing 50 to 60 gallons a year. He is reported to have said, "Except bark, opium and mercury, I believe no one medicine in the materia medica is likely to be of better service." Later, following work in Germany, it was used against diseases related to malnutrition, but nobody knew why it worked!

Early cod liver oil was produced by a 'rotting' process, the livers being taken out of the fish and left in a barrel until the oil separated. The resultant oil was dark in colour with a nauseatingly fishy smell and revolting taste. From about 1850 the livers were heated with steam which gave a higher yield and a paler coloured oil, that was still less than tasty. By the 1920s it was recognised that cod liver oil contained vital ingredients for healthy living, namely Vitamins A and D and polyunsaturated fats; it was therefore recommended as a preventative medicine, rather than as a cure.

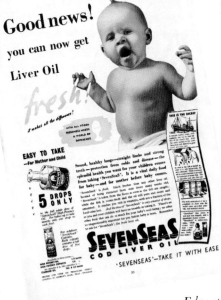

Educating the nation.. how Seven Seas promoted cod liver oil in 1938

During the 1930s, among the many trawling companies operating out of Hull, were the Boyd Line Ltd, Hudson Brothers Ltd, and Hellyer Brothers Ltd. These trawlermen experimented with boiling the livers at sea, whilst they were still fresh; some of the resultant oil was of high quality, certainly good enough for veterinary oil, possibly good even for medicinal use.

Once the oil had been drained into storage tanks, below the water line, where it was kept fresh by the proximity of the icy Arctic waters, it was sampled to establish its quality and determine the degree of further refining necessary. Most of this early processing was carried out by the Hull Fish Meal Company, but some far-sighted trawler owners, including Owen Hellyer and Tom Boyd formed the British Cod Liver Oil Producers (Hull) Ltd, a co-operative for the benefit of all the trawling fleets processing and selling oil on a central basis. Owen Hellyer, a great entrepreneur, became its first chairman. There was much to learn and others offered particular skills, such as Ernest Dawson who had experience of the cod liver oil industry and took on day to day management, and John and Charles Spencer; all three came from Isaac Spencer & Co (Aberdeen) Ltd. John F Ward, a chemist from Crookes Laboratories, and Professor John Drummond, an authority on vitamins and the chemistry of fats, also joined the team.

Various qualities of oil were produced, ranging from a lubricant used in the rolling of steel

Daily rations of cod liver oil being administered in a Second World War nursery; right, King Cod

to one for tanning hides into leather, whilst other grades were used in animal feeds. The new company, however, was particularly interested in the development of high quality veterinary oils and also ones suitable for medicinal purposes, but this required a new factory where the oil could be processed if necessary to make it paler, clarified by means of a centrifugal machine and deodorised to make it more acceptable. This factory was opened at Marfleet in 1935 – it was the world's largest cod liver oil refinery.

Ernest Dawson had made contact with Spillers, Spratts, Levers and Bibbys – makers of dog biscuits and animal feeds – but no real marketing policies existed, certainly none that enabled them to reach the manufacturers of drugs and medicinal products. It was eventually decided to market their products under the trade name of Solvitax.

By late 1935 medicinal quality cod liver oil was being produced but it had to conform to British Standards, with a vitamin potency of 600A and 85D units; the United States wanted 850A and 85D. Initially the cod liver oil was sold in 25 gallon tinplate drums enclosed in normal convex shaped wooden barrels, which added to the weight and volume of the package, incurring enormously high freight charges. This sys-

tem was subsequently replaced by ordinary steel drums which had a tin-coated inner surface; they were available in a variety of sizes, including a smaller one gallon container for the benefit of the general public.

When Owen Hellyer retired his place was taken by Kenneth MacLennan, from Lever Brothers, an expert on vitamin technology. He certainly brought enthusiasm to the company and encouraged new ideas. One such idea came when Hull Corporation sponsored a procession of decorated vehicles. Why not mount a giant cod on one of their vehicles? A carpenter was brought in, a few pounds of coloured canvas, paper, wood and string were bought and this large fish was created, complete with a microphone in its mouth, to relay a sales message – it was named King Cod! It proved an outstanding attraction and appeared at agricultural shows and other events up and down the country.

But Kenneth MacLennan knew that the future lay in standardisation and it was his decision to pack cod liver oil in small bottles for medicinal use, and to advertise it nationally. Before that could happen an easily recognisable brand name was needed and he suggested 'Seven Seas' and also 'Mainstay', for supplying trade. When Kenneth put the idea to Tom Boyd that they should manufacture cod liver oil in capsules he thought Tom was going to fire him instantly – he said, "We've got thousands of tons of cod liver oil to sell and, instead of our customers taking it by the dessert-spoon you want them to take it in these tiny pills".

During the Second World War the Ministry of Food established a scheme to provide children up to five, and pregnant and nursing women, with free supplies of cod liver oil. This created a demand that Hull and nearby Grimsby could not meet and oil had to be imported from Iceland and processed at Marfleet. These supplies were issued through the health clinics, and empty bottles were returned to the factory where they were re-filled by a work-force of 400 girls.

In the post-war years demand for their products grew as cod liver oil had helped produce a generation of healthy young children during the war years. Marketing also increased by participating in events like the Ideal Home Exhibition and similar trade fairs abroad. Distributors sent photographs showing stands in places like Lebanon, Australia and the Caribbean, for display in 'The Cod End', the house magazine. At last Seven Seas was becoming a household name, not only in Britain but all over the world.

Above, a 1960s range from Seven Seas; below, Marfleet Refinery

The company was always seeking to diversify and as a result of hydrogenating (hardening) it was possible to use oil in the manufacture of margarine. This led to a product called 'Morh', derived from the Latin for cod (Gaddus morrhuae), which was supplied to margarine and biscuit manufacturers, margarine being 50% fish oil. Other developments led to the importing of vegetable oils and the company changed its name to Marfleet Refining Company. In the early 1960s it was discovered that cod liver oil might be used in the treatment of tuberculosis and also in the reduction of blood cholesterol levels; it was also recognised that it was helpful in the prevention of gallstones, the healing of burns and wounds, treatment of certain types of arthritis and the care of the skin. Taste was still a major concern, impeding even bigger sales, but this improved with the introduction of hermetic refinery equipment. The finished oil remained clear in cold conditions, was almost tasteless and had a higher polyunsaturate content.

Today Seven Seas Ltd bottle 33,500 capsules of cod liver oil per minute and these are sold in 106 countries worldwide. Because of the restrictions of fishing only a small percentage of the crude oil comes from British trawlers. Outside the health care field Seven Seas Limited now supplies specialist products to the leather tanning, rubber, plastics, paint, lubrication and allied industries.

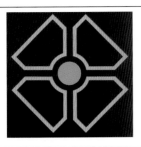

Sheffield Forgemasters Group

The early years of the 19th century were important for the steel industry, for Joseph Whitworth, Edward Vickers, William Armstrong, John Brown and Mark Firth were all born in its first two decades – all were destined to play a major role in the development of steel making.

Joseph Whitworth was born in Stockport and commenced in business in 1833 – from 1841 Whitworth's name would evermore become associated with the measurement of screw threads as the Whitworth thread was adopted as the standard for Great Britain. His firm grew and in 1860 he started to manufacture iron armour plate, in later years he took out patents for forging gun barrels from hollow steel ingots, and for making 'Whitworth Steel'.

William George Armstrong who was born in Newcastle was initially articled to a solicitor but turned to engineering in the 1840s. In 1847 he founded W G Armstrong & Co and built his works at Elswick in Newcastle. Within three years he was employing 300 people and in 1855 produced his first gun, a three pounder, and delivered it to the War Office. He later produced larger guns and in 1858 was appointed Engineer of Rifled Ordnance to the War Office with control over Woolwich Arsenal. In 1867 it was agreed that Armstrong's would build naval vessels at Mitchell's yard at Low Walker, Newcastle-upon-Tyne, and by 1881 they were employing 4000 people. A shipyard and steelworks was constructed for Sir W G Armstrong Mitchell & Co, the merged company, and by 1890 Armstrong's steelworks was producing 4000 tons of forgings and 2000 tons of castings a year.

In 1897 Armstrong purchased Joseph Whitworth & Co to form Armstrong Whitworth, and the new company built an armour plate mill at Openshaw, near Manchester. Some members of the Vickers family were already involved in iron and steel in the 1750s but it was Edward Vickers, initially a miller, who was really the founder of the modern Vickers company. He married the daughter of George Naylor, senior partner in the firm of Naylor & Sanderson, an iron and steel company in Sheffield. When this company was dissolved for family reasons, one of its successors was Naylor, Hutchinson, Vickers & Company – the Naylor was George's son, George Portus Naylor; the Vickers was Edward's brother,

Left, Edward Vickers; right, the Old Cutler's Hall, Sheffield

William Vickers, who also owned a rolling mill. This new firm began their steel business at Mill Sands Works and at Wadsley Bridge.

Edward gradually withdrew from milling and took on a dominant role in Naylor Vickers, as the company had become in 1841; later it became simply 'Vickers'. Ernst Benzon, a young German, became agent for Naylor Vickers in New York; in the rapidly expanding American markets he was able to stimulate a lot of trade in bars and sheets of steel, which were used to manufacture tools – he was not a manufacturer, but a keen businessman. While railway development in the United States was rapid at this time it was not without its risks as many of the pioneering companies overstretched themselves and could not pay their bills, but the company gained in prosperity and in 1863 they bought a plot of land on which was built the nucleus of the present River Don Works, Sheffield.

Tom Vickers, Edward's eldest son, although only 22, took over the running of the business from his father in 1856 – a man of determination he literally worked day and night. Under licence from a German company, Vickers started to manufacture bells in 1860 and Tom took out a patent for the manufacture of railway engine and carriage wheels made of cast steel. In 1867 Vickers became a limited company, half the shares being spread between Edward, his four sons and an employee, and the other half to Benzon who became chairman. Benzon died in 1873 and Tom Vickers then became chairman, a position he held for the next 35 years!

By the end of the century the works covered forty acres and were equipped with some of the best and most powerful plant in the steel industry. Already Vickers name was associated with armour plates for warships, finished guns, propellers, railway tyres and axles. In 1928 two great Sheffield companies, Vickers Ltd and Armstrong Whitworth, came together and formed Vickers Armstrong Ltd.

Across in Hull Charles Cammell was born in 1810, whilst William Laird came from Birkenhead. William Laird & Sons started shipbuilding in 1828. Charles Cammell moved to Sheffield in 1830 and along with two others founded Johnson Cammell & Co, file and steel manufacturers, in 1837. In 1845 the company moved to the newly built Cyclops Works, one of only two works in Sheffield to have their own railway sidings. In 1861 Cammell's began the manufacture of steel rails and the Pennsylvania Railroad Company agreed to use them, giving the company its first trade with the United States. By 1864 they were a limited liability company and had acquired the Yorkshire Iron & Steel Works at Penistone for the manufacture of steel rails, axles, locomotive and carriage tyres. In 1876 the company rolled the largest plate rolled so far – 18 feet by 5 feet by 22 inches, it weighed 35 tons! Less

Left, a 90-tonne arc furnace

than two decades later the Penistone works were shipping 2000 tons of rail to the United States each week; by the turn of the century Cammell's were employing 10,000 people.

In 1856 John Laird built a new shipyard, on the site of the present Cammell Lairds; in the next decade Laird Bros started a long tradition as shipbuilders to the Royal Navy but it wasn't until 1903 that the famous Cammell Laird & Co was formed.

Parallel to these developments John Brown started work in 1837 on his own account in Sheffield, later moving to larger works which he renamed Atlas Steel Works. In 1848 he started making springs and he invented the conical spring buffer. Later the company rolled a 5 ton armour plate and in 1863 erected a new armour mill plate plant which was capable of producing 12 inch thick armour plate.

Above, a propeller shaft for a nuclear ice breaker

In 1865 and 1866 John Brown was Master Cutler, and in 1868 he received a knighthood. Towards the close of the century the company developed all-steel armour plate and they erected a 10,000 ton armour forging press, an armour rolling mill and an 8,000 ton armour bending press.

John Brown & Co Ltd acquired a controlling interest in Thomas Firth & Sons Ltd, a company that had grown from small beginnings when Mark Firth had married Sarah Bingham in 1841, the daughter of a Sheffield scissor manufacturer. Thomas and his sons, Mark and Thomas, founded Thomas Firth & Sons at Portabello Steel Works. In 1856 they opened the first mill to roll steel for crinoline skirt frames as well as opening a new iron foundry at Chesterfield and other works for making heavy guns. Mark Firth also became Master Cutler and was Lord Mayor of Sheffield in 1875.

Chromium steel was first made at the Atlas Works in 1871, the first in England. By 1876 Thos. Firth & Sons was producing 100 ton guns for Italian vessels and early in the new century they started to manufacture engineers' tools and rock drills, turbine castings for liners, and also acquired works in Russia. By 1918 they had erected the well known Tinsley Works and had become major producers of stainless steel.

In 1929 Vickers Armstrong and Cammell Laird joined to form the English Steel Corporation and the following year Thomas Firth and part of John Brown & Co amalgamated to form Thomas Firth & John Brown Ltd.

In 1949 the industry was nationalised, although later returned to private ownership. Once again, following a return to Labour government, the British Steel Corporation was formed in 1967, but the next decade was one of gloom as the nationalised industry lost money and plants closed.

Sheffield Forgemasters Ltd was formed in 1982 as a joint venture between Johnson Firth Brown and the British Steel Corporation (River Don Works). In 1988 there was a management buyout which led to two-divisional structure, Engineering and Aerospace. A secondary management buyout was staged in 1996. Sheffield Forgemasters Ltd is currently the United Kingdom's leading privately owned specialist engineering company.

Silver Cross

Twenty-one year old William Wilson moved from Sunderland to Leeds to work as a perambulator springsmith. Some years later, in 1877, he started his own business as a pram manufacturer in small premises in Hunslet, Leeds.

William was a prolific inventor and he held more than 30 patents, which included such devices as an improved double suspension hammock, folding shafts for mail carts and a convertible mailcart – they all led to a steady and continuous growth for the business.

His first factory was in Silver Cross Street, Leeds, but in 1898 a new factory was built in Whitehouse Street. This one was was destroyed by fire a year later and although this seemed to be a disaster, the first Silver Cross Works were built on the same site.

In 1936, when the company was in the hands of the founder's three sons, Alfred, James and Irwin, it made its final move to its present headquarters and works at Guiseley, a few miles outside Leeds. At that time there were many pram manufacturers throughout the British Isles.

During the Second World War the Wilsons found themselves involved in the war effort, although this had its long term benefits for the work led them to develop new techniques for the manipulation of aluminium.

After the war the founder's grandsons, Lawrence Noble Wil-

Changes in Silver Cross pram design from the 1890s to the 1950s

son and William Noble Wilson took over the management of the company, and from their wartime experience with aluminum aircraft parts, they were able to develop new methods of manufacturing baby carriages. The company bought two special rubber hydraulic presses to produce side and end panels from aluminium sheet and introduced the latest paint re-flow process, originally developed for the motor industry. They also introduced tanks which contained copper, nickel and chromium in which the perambulators were immersed resulting in a high quality finish which set a new standard for the industry.

Quality has always been their keynote and for many years a Rolls Royce appeared in their advertisements. Lawrence Wilson, William's grandson, who served the company for 50 years, and became chairman and managing director, said: "Rolls Royce engines are the acme of engineering. It is my aim that our products shall be synonymous with the very best, the finest there is among baby carriages."

To mark the creation of an ambitious and expensive range of luxury baby carriages the trade name 'Wilson' was added to the famous 'Silver Cross' brand in 1957. By the early 1960s the company had started to diversify into making folding pushchairs. This decade also saw the production of baby carriage bodies in zinc coated steel, rather than aluminium, and the introduction of an automatic chromium plating plant. The 'Wilson' brand name remained strong until 1976 when it was decided to use only 'Silver Cross'. In 1988 the company changed its name from Lawrence Wilson &

Son Ltd to Silver Cross Ltd.

The company continues to hold fast to its long and valued reputation for style and quality. Each year about 30,000 baby carriages of all types are produced at Guiseley and many of these are exported to countries such as Ireland, Denmark, Spain, Norway, Germany, Australia and the United States. To support their export market in Ireland, Silver Cross (Ireland) Ltd has been formed with responsibilities for marketing and distribution of the Silver Cross range through the Republic of Ireland and Ulster.

1997 was the company's 120th anniversary and Silver Cross is proud to be one of the first manufacturers to feature on the Internet. The company has recently established a retail outlet at West Side Retail Park in Guiseley, one of the finest nursery shops in the North of England.

Smith+Nephew

Thomas James Smith opened his chemist's shop in the old town area of Hull in 1856, and described himself as an 'Analytical and Pharmaceutical Chemist'. He was thirty years old and a member of the newly formed British Pharmaceutical Society, extremely interested in medicine, and his work was eventually to see him become a wholesale supplier to hospitals, particularly of cod liver oil.

The cod liver oil of those days was dark brown in colour with a strong fishy flavour, but he worked hard refining and blending the oil to produce a more palatable medicine. In 1875 he sold over £3,000 worth of cod liver oil and in 1883 he won a gold medal for the quality of his oil at an International Fisheries Exhibition. Already he was supplying such institutions as Guy's and Great Ormond Street Hospitals. As a minor part of his business he also supplied bandages and wound dressings.

The business was, however, still a small one and at no time did he employ more than three people – indeed for many years he was his own sales representative. In 1896, by now almost 70 years old and in poor health, he invited his nephew, Horatio Nelson Smith, aged 22, to join the company and in July of that year T J Smith & Nephew came into existence.

Three months later Thomas died, leaving his half share of the business to his sister, Amelia Ann. However, a few years later she decided to transfer this share to Horatio, together with all the furniture in the house, in exchange for an annuity of £260 during her lifetime. This rather strange transaction was not witnessed by a lawyer but by the family doctor! It gave Horatio full control of the business.

Horatio had worked for a wholesale draper and woollen manufacturer in London and had acquired a knowledge of textile manufacturing. This training in textiles now began to make its mark on the company. He bought a machine from Germany for cutting and rolling bandages and purchased cloth from Lancashire. Ever an enthusiastic traveller he set off for North America in 1906 to secure overseas business and won contracts to supply Canadian hospitals with bandages.

In 1907 the firm became a limited company

Left, Horatio Nelson Smith; above, the founder, T J Smith

with a paid up capital of £207, and having outgrown its premises in North Churchside moved to a larger building at 5 Neptune Street, Hull, bought for £2,000. In 1912 the company saw its first expansion with the purchase of a sanitary towel manufacturing business.

Smith & Nephew had already supplied the Turks in their conflict with Italy and was well-placed to meet the enormous demands placed upon it by the fighting in the First World War.

To meet ever increasing needs the company opened a manufacturing plant in Canada and also purchased a textile mill in Lancashire – at the beginning of the war they had 50 employees, at its end they had 1,200!

However such growth also brought its problems when warfare ended and a fallback in trade occurred. Soon staff numbers had also fallen back, to 183! Horatio quickly tackled the problems with more overseas sales drives and in 1921 the first Smith & Nephew independent overseas branch was opened in Canada.

In 1924 an Act was passed which called for the provision of First Aid equipment in industrial and commercial premises in the United Kingdom. To satisfy such requirements Smith & Nephew introduced its own range of First Aid Kits. Horatio also bought into revolutionary new processes, one being Elastoplast, an elastic adhesive fabric which soon revolutionised the treatment of varicose ulcers, and has become one of the world's leading support bandages. It developed into a range of individual dressings and today millions are produced each week in the United Kingdom and other parts of the world. Elastoplast is often regarded as a generic name for sticking plasters but is a trade mark of Smith & Nephew; in certain other countries it is sold under the name of Tensoplast. The other process was a commercially produced quality plaster of Paris.

By 1937 new product development was forging ahead and Smith & Nephew Associated Companies Ltd, a new public company, was formed. However once again war clouds were gathering and the company worked with the government to ensure stocks of wound dressings were at a satisfactory level, but demand for Elastoplast soon outstripped supplies.

After the war the company developed a network of new overseas companies, agencies and distributors, and a programme of factory mod-ernisation was also commenced.

In 1951 Herts Pharmaceuticals was acquired, bringing to the company pharmaceutical products and cosmetic creams, but also laboratories and staff which provided the basis of Smith & Nephew Research Company, an important part of the present day company. Horatio Nelson Smith lived until he was 86, and died in 1960, having been chairman of the Board until 1954.

In 1983 an important new acquisition took place when Rolyan, based in Wisconsin, brought into the group its low temperature thermoplastic splinting materials and rehabilitation aids. Similarly in 1986 another United States company Richards Medical was purchased, bringing to the company trade in surgical implants and joint reconstruction devices, and instrumentation for arthroscopy and microsurgery.

Today Smith & Nephew is a leading world healthcare company which employs over 12,000 people in more than 30 countries. In 1995 the Medical Division, based in Hull, received the Queen's Award for Export. The company now manufactures several hundred medical products, many being used in hospitals throughout the world.

James Greenhalgh was a Yorkshire wholesale draper based in Huddersfield. Ever an entrepreneur, he saw that there was money to be made by selling fireworks in the weeks running up to the 5th November. Most of his supplies were made by outworkers, mainly coal miners wishing to supplement their income, although some supplies came from China. These arrived at east coast ports before being brought to Huddersfield by barge.

James started his business in 1891, but before this, in south west Scotland, Charles Brock had started manufacturing fireworks prior to 1720, and was also a major player in the formulation of the Explosives Act of 1875. The Act was the first real legislation in this area and is still an important piece of legislation. The firm of Brock's became part of Standard fireworks in 1987.

Edward, Richard, Kate and Ruth, James' four children (there was actually a twenty year gap between Edward and Richard!), eventually

Above, James and Martha Greenhalgh with their children Kate and Edward (back) and Ruth and Richard; right, the programme for the 1924 firework display at Crystal Palace. In 1986 Brock's became part of Standard Fireworks

became involved in the business and initially a small factory was opened at Rowley Hill, Lepton, near Huddersfield, before a disused stone quarry at Crosland Hill became the company's home in 1910. The quarry was an ideal site as it was spacious and had gunpowder stores which had been used by the previous owners!

Unfortunately the growth of the company was delayed by the First World War but during those years they diverted to producing hand grenades and other items for the war effort. After the war they were able to concentrate on the production of fireworks again and although the depression had an effect, business remained buoyant until the outbreak of the Second World War. That year's 5th November displays were already manufactured for sale but they had to be put into storage until hostilities ended in 1945! This time war work was slow to materialise and most of the staff had to be laid off but later the company helped the war effort with the production of blackout blinds and blackout lampshades, as well

at Sanquhar was disposed of. From 1987 a much more aggressive attitude towards marketing was adopted and by the end of 1990 business had almost doubled.

After a management buyout in 1992 the company reverted to private ownership, with Mel Barker as managing director. Today it is the only remaining family firework manufacturer in the United Kingdom and may well be the largest manufacturer in Europe. As well as supplying hundreds of thousands of families with their 5th November displays Standard Fireworks arranges summer displays, in conjunction with symphony orchestras, at stately homes such as Harewood House and Nostell Priory. The company still employs over 300 people, a high proportion of them being women, and many of these are employed in South Yorkshire where the company sponsors the South Elmsall Colliery Brass Band.

Standard Fireworks produce 75% of all the fireworks they sell, and although some still come from China they have to meet the safety requirements of the United Kingdom.

as making flares and decoy bullets.

In 1945 the stored fireworks were allowed to light up the skies over Britain, and appeared none the worse for their period of storage. As expansion took place there was great competition for staff with the textile mills and it was necessary to look for staff from further afield. The mining communities of South Yorkshire provided the answer – there was plenty of work for men but little for the women. These women proved ideal for an industry heavily dependent on people with nimble fingers, very little of it being mechanised. Factories were therefore opened in South Elmsall and South Kirkby.

In 1959 the company was floated on the stock market but the Greenhalghs carried on running the business. Edward, Richard and Kate were now joined by Frederick Rowcliffe, Ruth's husband, and Richard's son, Barry.

In June 1986 the company was taken over by Scottish Heritable Trust and the following year they bought out Brock's Fireworks Ltd. In 1988 the military pyrotechnics arm of Brock's was sold off and the Scottish factory

Top, early days in Huddersfield; right, part of a Standard Fireworks poster

The origins of Terry's go back to 1767 when Mr Bayldon and Mr Berry, who were importers of citrus peel and made confectionery near to Bootham Bar in York, entered into partnership. They were joined, and finally succeeded, by Joseph Terry who was the firm's true founder. Joseph Terry was born in York in 1793, the son of a farmer, but he served an apprenticeship and became an apothecary. Joseph opened his shop in Walmgate and there he learnt the useful art of 'sugaring the pill'. He was the forerunner of the modern pharmacist, but was also jack-of-all-trades, as medicine was still in its early days.

In 1823 Joseph married Harriet Atkinson, who was related to Berry, and it may have been as a result of this that Joseph left Walmgate and joined the two partners. The following year they moved from Bootham Bar to St. Helen's Square, in the centre of York. By 1825 Bayldon had dropped out, Robert Berry had died, and his son and Joseph became partners, using the name Terry and Berry. They were also joined by a Mr. Coultherd, but both he and Mr Berry had retired by the end of the decade.

Joseph Terry, apothecary, baker, confectioner and peel importer was now on his

A wholesale price list, including a wide variety of fruit drops and similar sweets priced at either 52/- or 36/- per cwt

own; his factory was in Brearley Yard and his 'front shop' was in St. Helen's Square, only a few yards away from the Mansion House. Soon he was establishing a reputation for cakes and comfits, sugar sweet, candied peel, marmalade, mushroom ketchup and medicated lozenges – the link between the chemist and the confectioner was retained!

At that time before anyone could practise a trade they had to buy their 'freedom', at a cost of £25 from the City Fathers, and to import goods they had to have a licence from the Merchant Adventurers at a further cost of £25. York was a bustling city and no doubt at the balls and in the 'withdrawing rooms' the ladies exchanged Joseph Terry's 'Conversation Lozenges' on which were impressed such coy opening gambits as 'Can you polka?!', 'How do you flirt?', and 'Love me'!

With the death of George III the city's fortunes waned but were reawakened with the coming of the railway in the 1840s. By this time Terry was sending his products, albeit in small quantities, to 75 towns spread throughout the north of England, into the Midlands and as far south as London, and they included jujubes, coltsfoot rock, acidulated drops, gum balls, and varied lozenges. Joseph Terry & Company was no longer a local supplier, but was on the way to gaining a national and international reputation. As early as 1836 Joseph Terry was among those other confectioners and lozenge makers who formed an association to protect the public 'against

Above, a decorated wedding cake from the 1920s; below a 1933 selection of chocolates

individuals manufacturing or vending lozenges and confectionery composed of injurious materials'.

When Joseph died in 1850, Joseph jnr carried on the business, although he was only 22. In 1854 Robert and John joined him and the firm became Joseph Terry & Sons.

However, of the three brothers, it was Joseph who was to be the driving force behind the company's development. Their supplies of sugar, cocoa, glucose, orange and lemon rinds in brine, and coal for the newly installed steam plant, all came to the city by steam-packet and so he leased a riverside site at Clementhorpe to house his stocks of peel. Soon Joseph Terry & Sons were displaying their wares at various national exhibitions and being awarded gold, silver and bronze medals – in 1899 they won a gold for confectionery at the National Temperance Catering Exhibition!

In 1886 Joseph Terry built a chocolate factory in Clementhorpe, although in his price list for 1867, which included over 400 separate items, only 13 of these were chocolate products. For many firms the making of chocolate to eat, as opposed to drink, was a development from cocoa; for Terry's it was a natural development to their range of confectionery.

Although a good businessman Joseph was also very civic-minded, serving as Sheriff of York, and also as Lord Mayor on four occasions, including Queen Victoria's Jubilee year, when he represented the city in the celebrations and was subsequently knighted for his work. The Yorkshire Herald said: "There was no person in the city more beloved and respected." It went on to expound his qualities, "not least his association with many of the religious and philanthropic institutions in the city..."

In 1895 the firm became Joseph Terry & Sons Ltd, with Sir Joseph and his son, Thomas Walker Leaper Terry, as governing directors. Rather late on in life Sir Joseph had married a second time, and had produced a second family, among them Frank, who would be chairman of the company for 35 years. When Sir Joseph died in 1895 he was succeeded by Thomas, who had been responsible for developing the early export trade; however he was killed in a motor accident in 1910.

A new generation came to the forefront; Frank joined

the firm in 1903, aged 25 and Noel joined eight years later at the age of 22. Chocolate was also growing in popularity, for in the War Office Times and Naval Review for Christmas 1905 it said: "Now chocolate is ... the sweetmeat of the Services.on the march, at manoeuvres, or on any special occasion where staying power is need-ed." Before the First World War Terry's produced their first assortment, 'Brit-annia'.

Just prior to the out-break of war Frank Terry went to Germany to study their production methods and brought back equip-ment for use at York; indeed throughout his chairmanship he led the company forward with the installation of modern equipment, providing they were still able to produce the best chocolate. During the war and in the early post war years H E Leetham, a flour miller, was chairman; Noel Terry was to marry his daughter. By about 1920 Terry's, realising the growing importance of chocolate, built a new factory especially for chocolate at Clementhorpe and here production started of such well known brands as Spartan in 1921, and All Gold in 1932.

Also in the early 1920s Frank and Noel Terry went to Venezuela to inspect the cocoa planta-tions, purchasing one to ensure the source of their prime raw material; another important pur-chase at this time was a site near the York race-course where they were to build their present factory – the Bishopthorpe Road site was a real statement of confidence in the future.

On the death of H E Leetham, Frank and Noel became joint managing directors. Noel had a strong belief in the need to advertise, in a period when advertising was not generally accepted. The company's vans became mobile display units, enabling the retailer to see the complete range of Terry's products. Noel also helped the company make the change from hand-written daybooks to machine recording and accounting, although the age of the computer was still a long way off!

Complementing Noel's work, Frank was regarded as the complete confectioner, his insistence on quality being uncompromising.

In 1936 he was knighted, and when a subscription was raised in the works for his portrait to be painted it was quickly over subscribed; to his worker he was 'The Boss' – the father-figure loved, respected and feared!

In 1945 he was appointed High Sheriff of Yorkshire. But the Second World War had brought difficul-ties, for part of the Bishopthorpe works had to also house F. Hills & Sons who made Jablo pro-peller blades, and Chivers & Sons, the jam-man-ufacturers, who stayed until 1954.

In the early 1960s Joseph Terry & Sons Ltd became part of Forte's (Holdings) Ltd. For almost two hundred years it had remained a family business, helped by a dedicated labour force where frequently father and son worked together, quite a number staying with the com-pany for fifty years or more. Over succeeding decades the ownership of Terry's has changed several times; in 1977 it became part of Colgate Palmolive, then came under the control of United Biscuits before passing to Philip Morris, and now it is in the hands of Kraft Jacobs Suchard, as Terry's Suchard.

JOSHUA TETLEY & SON BREWERY

Joshua Tetley was born in 1778, fourth of the eight children of William and Elizabeth Tetley. William was a successful maltster in Armley, which was then a village on the outskirts of Leeds, and it is believed that Elizabeth's father was a successful businessman for they had a London address, as well as one in Leeds. Sadly, on Christmas Eve 1788, Elizabeth died aged 36. William now had responsibility for bringing up their six boys, the youngest was three, the eldest fourteen, as well as running a business, but Lucy Rimington, Elizabeth's sister, now came to run the home.

The family business went through times of success, but also times when bankruptcy seemed inevitable. In 1783, England suffered rampant inflation, through its involvement in the American War of Independence. This led to price increases in barley and wheat, described by the Mayor of Leeds as being 'so exorbitant that it almost amounts to a prohibition on the use of it'. Such increases led to a decline in the sales of beer and therefore in the demand for his malt. However two years later William bought 24 acres of land, which made him one of the biggest landowners in Armley. The see-saw effect continued and whilst in 1798 malt cost 4s 9d a bushel, in 1800 it cost 9s 2d; similarly a 4lb loaf of bread in 1794 cost 7½d, in 1800 it cost 17½d – such changes brought chains of bankruptcies as one business put pressure on another. William Tetley was one of the victims and in spite of Lucy Rimington lending him £2,000 a petition for bankruptcy was served on him in April 1800. William was determined to repay all he owed and by disposing of everything, except his home and the maltings (although he sold some of his furniture), he received clearance from bankruptcy in October 1800.

In 1801 William Tetley & Sons was formed and traded in malt, wines and spirits, serving customers in various parts of the country; they also became agents for the Imperial Fire Insurance Office of London. The 'lads', as he called them, were not all employed in the central business. They were sent out like merchant adventurers to establish themselves, but linked back to the core by trading, perhaps a lesson learned from the bankruptcy. As a teenager Joshua Tetley

Left, Joshua Tetley; below, an early drawing of his brewery

Above, the first pub Tetley bought, the Duke William, now closed but forming part of the Brewery Wharf Visitor Centre. This photo shows Bernard and Emma Giles, tenants from 1904 to 1932

helped in the family business and when he was 29 he married Hannah Carbutt, aged 23, the daughter of a linen and cloth merchant of Leeds. From the diary jottings of Elizabeth, Joshua's daughter, we gather that he was a shy retiring man, whose opinions were valued but who avoided the limelight, so much so that only on two occasions would he let his likeness be drawn. From other sources we know that Joshua and his family were regular worshippers at Christ Church, Meadow Lane, Leeds where he was one of the first churchwardens.

Joshua and Hannah's first home was in Albion Street, Leeds – a good address, but not in the area of the gentry. There they had five children, all girls, but the longed-for boy, Francis William, was not born until 1817 after they had moved to fashionable Park Square, to

be followed by yet another two girls. Only Francis William, and Sarah, the fourth daughter, married. In the 1817 Baines Leeds Directory Joshua Tetley is listed, at Park Square, as a British Wine Merchant – presumably he operated from their home at Mill Hill but had no business address.

When Joshua bought a small brewery belonging to his friend and maltings customer, William Sykes, in 1822 the family moved to live at the brewery house in Salem Place. At that time the working people of the city had little money and existed on bread and beer, beer being much safer to drink than the often polluted water piped to houses in central Leeds. However Joshua was fortunate, for the brewery had its own bore-hole, which gave pure water, rich in minerals.

Buying the right brewery was important but

it was equally important to employ the best possible brewer; Joshua chose a Mr Giles. Joshua leased Sykes Brewery buildings and bought the 30-year-old business for £400. His first year, as expected, was a poor one, for it took time for a new product to become known by word of mouth, and accepted. However to ensure his financial safety he kept his own malt business going, selling to innkeepers and private houses who brewed their own beer; he also sold flour.

1830 was a significant year for the brewing industry for two very different reasons. Firstly, the Beer House Act made it legal for anyone paying a two guinea fee to sell beer without needing the permission of the Justices. The new beer houses, known as Tom and Jerry shops, were able to remain open from 4am to 10pm. Secondly, the first English Temperance Society was formed in Bradford in February 1830, with its constitution stating that members 'abstain from distilled spirits'.

Joshua had to play an increasing role in the running of William Tetley & Sons as his father was now about 80 years old and Joshua's brother William who had run the business died in 1831. When old William died in 1834 the estate was left to William and Joshua, but as William had already died the whole estate, valued at about £450, went to Joshua.

Hunt where you will —

TETLEY'S ALES

Are first in the field

1834 was the year the railway came to Leeds; trains ran to Selby to join up with the steam packet service from Hull. The coming of the railways was an important factor in the success story of Joshua Tetley. He always believed that 'Quality Pays' and whilst he insisted that his products should be of the best quality, he also insisted that whatever he purchased should also be of that quality. As his business expanded he moved to live at Belmont House, Little Woodhouse, a most desirable property, and about the same time took his 21-year-old son Francis William into partnership, the company becoming Joshua Tetley & Son; in the indenture of partnership they were both described as common brewers and maltsters. From its small beginnings the property in 1841 was valued at £30,842.

In 1847 Francis William Tetley married Isabella Maxwell Ryder, the daughter of Arthur Ryder of London, who for many years had been a business contact of Tetleys. Now there was no need to worry about succession, for the couple's first child was a boy, Charles Francis; they had a further six boys and seven girls — there was 25 years between the eldest and youngest!

About 1850, with trade expanding at a rapid rate, the company bought land adjoining the old

Centre, loading up the bottled beer at the turn of the century; left early use of the Huntsman logo

Sykes Brewery, which was still only leased. They anticipated the need to extend the premises and in 1852 work commenced; by 1875 the company was producing up to 171,500 barrels of ale and porter a year. However these provincial breweries were very small compared with ones in London. From the 1850s Joshua Tetley, now in his 70s, had a decreasing involvement in the business and only took £600 a year 'in lieu of profits'. In 1856 he went to live in the Hollings, a country mansion, at Hampsthwaite, near Harrogate. His wife died the following year and Joshua died in 1859; both are buried in Hampsthwaite churchyard.

Graham Simpson became only the 12th head brewer in the company's 175-year history

The malting business continued until 1861. By this time the beer trade had grown so much that the brewery needed all the malt they could produce. The deliveries of malt were replaced by deliveries of beer, often using the new railway system and the agents which Tetleys had set up in London, Liverpool and Manchester.

Although Francis William was only 41, his health was not good and he took his brother-in-law, Charles Ryder, into partnership; Charles Francis Tetley was at that time only 10 years old. Joshua Tetley & Son were now in a strong

financial position and in 1864 they bought the Old Sykes Brewery and started to rebuild the premises. It involved the creation of large cellars, a hop store and a 'stone-room' (where the fermenting took place).

The company's first trademark, a shield with a lion rampant in a five-pointed star, appeared in June 1859 and was used until 1921 when the famous Tetley huntsman appeared. In 1860 they introduced a show-card advertising India Pale Ale Imperial (a strong barley wine) which incorporated the Leeds coat of arms. At this time opening hours of public houses were liberal – all publicans should close their houses from 1am to 4am!

It became increasingly important that young Charles Francis Tetley should be properly educated and prepared for leadership and management. At the age of ten he had been sent to Leeds Grammar School; later he moved to Harrow and Trinity College, Cambridge; he was also kept in contact with the firm before going to two leading brewers away from the family business to gain experience – he was 29 before he was made a partner. By the 1880s many breweries were buying up public houses and 'tying' them to their own brands of beer; Tetleys were reluctant to do this but gradually saw their outlets diminish. In 1890 they had two tied houses, the Duke William which was alongside the brewery and the Fleece at Farsley, but soon many others were purchased, albeit with great care to ensure they gave value for money!

Tetleys started experiments in bottling beers and stouts in 1892 and two years later its boom led to further extensions to the works. To finance all these purchases and extensions the brewery became a private limited company, Joshua Tetley & Son Ltd, in 1897, but all the share capital was retained by the three directors.

In 1899 a Royal Commission on Liquor Licensing Laws sought to obtain a large reduction in the number of outlets for strong drink and the 1904 Licensing Act laid down that public houses should be closed where they were surplus to the requirements of an area; between 1900 and 1914 the number of public houses fell from 102,189 to 87,660. However this was a period of general trade decline and no doubt the compensation received helped to pay the loans outstanding on the premises bought a few years earlier by the breweries. During the First World War beer consumption in Britain fell from about 37 million barrels to 19 million, the result of the Defence of the Realm Act, which curtailed opening hours, and also the heavy duty imposed on beer, but Tetleys bucked the trend and their profits rose sharply.

In those early years of the new century it was usual for the horse drays to go to towns as far distant as Harrogate on a Monday. The drayman would then collect beer each day from the railway station and deliver it to pubs in the locality, before returning to the brewery on Friday. In 1912 the brewery bought a Yorkshire Patent Steam Wagon, the first step towards modern methods of transportation. Another innovation came in 1916 when the brewery employed women for the first time; they worked in the maltings.

Between the wars the sales of beer in Britain often fluctuated with the fall and rise of the economy. Tetleys expanded in Lancashire in the 1930s with the purchase of public houses and off licences, and also spread into North Wales, Cheshire and the Lake District.

After the Second World War Tetleys bought further outlets and embarked on a number of mergers, among them one with Walker Cain Ltd in 1960 which gave them ownership of 2771 licensed properties and an issued share capital of over

£16 million. During this period Tetleys also embarked on a major modernisation of the maltings and the brewhouse. In 1961 Tetley Walker, Ind Coope, and Ansells came together, and the following year changed their name to Allied Breweries Ltd. Following the acquisition in 1978 of J Lyons & Co Ltd, the food and beverage company, the name became Allied-Lyons plc in 1981. In 1993 Carlsberg-Tetley was formed from a merger between Allied Breweries and Carlsberg UK; in 1997 Carlsberg A/S in Denmark became the majority shareholder of Carlsberg-Tetley.

The Tetley story would be incomplete without mention of the shire horses, part of the brewery's public image and regularly seen at attractions throughout the county, magnificently turned-out, synonymous with the quality beers the brewery produces. Tetleys' heritage and production processes are now best seen at the Brewery Wharf Visitor Centre. 1997 celebrates 175 years of the Joshua Tetley & Son brewery, and of 'Quality Pays'.

Tetley shire horses still make occasional deliveries

Robert Thompson was born in 1876, the son of John and Dinah Thompson, in the lovely village of Kilburn in the Hambleton Hills, north of York.

Apparently he was a bright lad and his father, the local joiner and wheelwright, was keen that Robert should leave the village and go to Cleckheaton in the West Riding of Yorkshire, some 50 miles away, to take up an engineering apprenticeship. He stayed there for five years but his heart was really back in his native village of Kilburn, not in the industrial textile town of Cleckheaton. During those five years he must often have passed through Ripon on his visits home and called in at the Cathedral.

Towards the end of the fifteenth century woodcarvers had carried out work of great beauty in the collegiate church of St. Peter and St. Wilfrid in Ripon, later to become Ripon Cathedral, and chief among these craftsmen was William Bromflet. Robert became inspired by Bromflet's artistry.

At the age of twenty, after pleading with his father, he returned to the family business, taking on the general joinery work of a rural community.

The craftsmanship that had inspired him in Ripon Cathedral had been done centuries ago but he believed that he could rekindle that spirit; he also wanted to work with English oak. In his spare time he read about the craftsmen of former years and about the properties of the wood that they had used; he also searched for those same traditional tools employed by the men that he so much admired.

To Robert, English oak became an obsession. He studied it in all its phases and decided that if it was to retain its qualities and character it must be allowed to season naturally, slowly, stacked in the open air, the time needed being determined by the thickness of the planks. Not for him the modern 'kiln drying' methods!

For several years he helped his father, saving

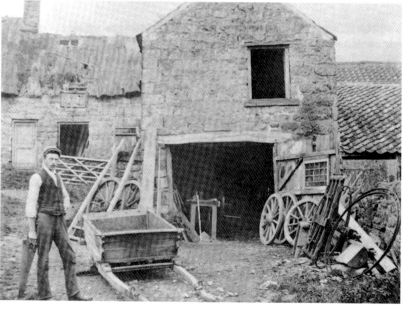

Above, Robert Thompson
and right, his first workshop
at Kilburn

Left, the Mouseman Visitor Centre at Kilburn; above, table tops are given a special effect by use of an adze; below, a craftsman carves the mouse trademark to a refectory table leg

money to buy his beloved oak so that he might lay it down to mature ready for the day when he could work it, fashion it for some particular purpose. In the meantime he took on extra tasks, among them stone carving. He carved a gargoyle on the tower of Gilling church and a stone war memorial tablet in the church at Thirsk. Gradually his remarkable carving skills, and his understanding of his basic materials (not only oak – he also used real cowhide and wrought iron) became recognised and he was asked to make a pulpit for Yearsley church and communion rails for the church at Harome.

In May 1919 Robert Thompson was visited by Father Paul Neville, who was soon to become headmaster of the Benedictine Abbey School at Ampleforth, seven miles from Kilburn. He came to ask Robert to make a large memorial cross for

Robert Thompson made this chair for York Minster during the war, in a period when he had no staff

This man of vision slowly gathered round him a team of craftsmen, but by 1925 this still only numbered six. To encourage them to produce their finest work he reminded them that their pieces would last for 300 years!

Robert Thompson always said that the choice of a mouse came about by accident, when Charlie Barker, one of his craftsmen, commented that for all their work they were still as "poor as Church mice". This appealed to Robert and, so the story goes, on the spur of the moment he carved a mouse in a beam.

A letter in Robert's handwriting dated 1949, however, suggests the mouse first appeared on the cornice of a screen. Whichever story is true, in 1931 the Trades Marks Journal published details of the mouse as being the trademark of Robert Thompson, Kilburn near York, describing him as an Ecclesiastical Contractor. A special mouse was carved to send to the Patent Office, and this was presented to George Bolton of Bradford who was his solicitor.

Robert thought that the busy little mouse, chewing away at a piece of solid oak, was symbolic of industry in quiet places; symbolic of his own situation!

Robert and his wife Ada had a daughter, Elsie, but no sons, and so the business was carried on by his grandsons, Robert and John Cartwright, and now by his great-grandsons. Robert Thompson died in 1955.

Today throughout the world, in famous churches but also in many homes, examples of the famous Mouseman craftsmanship take pride of place, and on each piece, somewhere, a small mouse can be found.

the Catholic cemetery at Ampleforth. This was the first of many commissions for the school and its church and gave him the chance to realise those dreams he had on his visits to Ripon.

One of the early tools he came across in his searchings was an adze, an axe-like tool which had its blade set at right angles to its handle, and was used to rough out the broad shapes on ships' timbers. He used it to give a tooled effect to the surfaces of his furniture, something which became a hallmark of his craftsmanship. But although the adzing was a feature of much of his work, it was the 'mouse' which became his trademark.

TUPGILL PARK STABLES

It has been suggested that the monks of Jervaulx were famous for horse breeding. It may be that the present day stables in Middleham, where about 300 racehorses are in training, owe their origins to those distant days.

Middleham is set in the far north of the county and is known for its strong air, stiff winds, and beautiful scenery. The now ruined castle eventually passed to Richard III. It may no longer be a noble residence but is a stepping stone in the history of the town and its link with the sport of kings.

The Middleham High and Low Moors provide ideal training grounds, galloping land, for the racehorses. As far back as the middle of the 18th century large numbers of racehorses were coming to Middleham and the town had a racecourse by 1739, laid out on High Moor, some of the highest ground in Wensleydale; it is still possible to see remains of it on the edge of the present day gallops. Records suggest that Isaac Cape was probably Middleham's first trainer, based at Tupgill from 1765. The last race on High Moor in was 1873.

The moor is common land and 'gaitowners', landowners who have grazing rights on the Moors, used to cause a problem by grazing live-

Right, Frederick Bates, as pictured in the Racing Illustrated of 1895; below, the Stables at Tupgill Park during the late 19th century

stock on the area. Today the local trainers generally have a financial arrangement with the gaitowners, which allow the Moors to be used for training without risk of injury of horses tripping in holes made by cattle.

Ever since those early days many famous racehorses have been trained at Middleham, including Theodore, which won the St. Leger in 1822; Dr. Syntax, trained at Tupgill, which won many Gold Cups, among them one run at Middleham; Wallace, which won the Goodwood Stakes in 1860; and the Derby winner Pretender of 1869. Pretender was trained by Fred Bates who was one of Tupgill Park's most famous and successful trainers in the 19th century. It wasn't until 1945 that Middleham had another Derby winner, Dante, trained by Matt Peacock.

Today the Tupgill Park stables are owned by Colin Armstrong, whose grandfather Bob Armstrong bought them in 1904, and who lived and trained there until his death in 1956. Bob Armstrong's sons both trained in adjacent stables – Gerald in Thorngill and Sam in Ashgill,

until he went to Newmarket in 1945, where he died in 1981, and where he is now succeeded by his son Robert.

Though Colin was never to be a trainer, over the last 24 years he has spent heavily, repairing the stables and returning them to their former glory. He has also landscaped Tupgill Park and built 'The Forbidden Corner' – the garden and grotto which are now open to the public and attract thousands of visitors each year.

The present trainers at Tupgill Park, Steve Kettlewell and Micky Hammond, have both been jockeys. Even in his early schooldays at Scorton, Steve knew what he wanted to be and rode his first winner, riding Lothian Brig at Newcastle, when only 17 years old. He turned to training in 1987. Micky Hammond was a jockey for ten years and during that time he won more than 230 races.

Mr Bates and two friends on the right watch a string of his horses in the shadow of Penhill

Waddingtons

John Waddington, a tall impressive man who wore a cavalry style moustache, was an apprentice printer. On completion of his apprenticeship he entered into a partnership with Wilson Barrett, an actor/manager at the Leeds Grand Theatre. The company was called Waddingtons Ltd. It was formed before 1900, and at that time they were colour printers, printing theatre posters and other advertising material for stage productions. Their premises were on Camp Road, not far from where Leeds University now stands.

It appears that John Waddington was a very difficult person and the partnership did not last long. John Waddington left the business and started on his own, but this business soon ran into money difficulties having to be rescued by Frederick Eley, manager of the local National Provincial Bank. Mr Eley suggested that a private limited company be formed, which was created in 1905. Among the shareholders was Fred Karno, a member of the theatrical world. John Waddington persuaded his fellow directors to buy lithographic equipment and resulting from this decision Victor Watson, a lithographer at Harrison Townsend, was appointed lithographic foreman.

Victor Watson was a dynamic character with great personality and energy. He quickly improved the quality of the printing and worked hard to obtain further orders. However John Waddington encountered money difficulties and in March 1913 he resigned. The other directors were inclined to close the business down but Watson persuaded them to keep it open and he was appointed manager. He was given six months to put the business on its feet but very quickly proved so successful that extra capacity had to be found and he rented a factory in Elland Road, near to the present home of Leeds United Football Club, but this was gutted by a fire on Good Friday 1915. By 10am the following morning he had heard that another printing business was for sale and by mid-day, tentative arrangements were made and he was able to make an immediate move and re-start the business. The machines started to turn on the Saturday afternoon, worked Sunday, Easter Monday and Tuesday. When the other staff returned to work on Wednesday they were amazed to see the new management and staff but Victor Watson was able to employ both workforces as some of the regular workers had joined the forces.

In 1916 Victor Watson was appointed a director. In 1919 the company joined the Master Printers' Federation and in 1920 the original Waddingtons Ltd, then a small business compared with the new company, was purchased and incorporated into the company. To enable the firm to gain extra capital the company went public in

John Waddington

1921. About this time photographic reproduction was leading to greatly improved printing. Waddingtons were asked by another printer to take on an order to print some chocolate box tops. To ensure the best quality Victor Watson sought the help of Achille Vauvelle, a Frenchman living in Britain, an expert in this recent development, and persuaded him to sign a contract to work exclusively for Waddingtons.

This was a major achievement.

In 1921 Victor Watson became joint managing director and Frederick Eley, now Sir Frederick, was appointed chairman. As a result of the company's growth a factory was bought at Hunslet, just inside the Leeds boundary. That year it was agreed to develop playing card manufacture. By now Waddingtons was a nationally known company, and through the playing cards it became known internationally.

A 1950 edition of Subbuteo

Victor Watson saw the need for the company to be recognised for a speciality work. He was a keen card player and saw how these could be produced during slack periods and be put into stock. Norman Watson, his elder son, now a member of the firm, strongly supported the idea. In 1922 Charles Goodall & Co Ltd had been absorbed by Thomas De La Rue & Co Ltd thus leaving only one other playing card manufacturer. During the First World War playing cards became very popular and were in great demand; an energetic approach was appropriate. It was essential that the backs of all the cards in a pack were identical, that cards were all exactly the same size and had the correct finish – the project was demanding! Soon Waddingtons were developing sponsored playing cards, incorporating an advertisement. These were the basis of Waddington's 'Beautiful Britain', ones subsidised by the Great Western Railway Company and later by the London & North Eastern Railway Company, cards depicting many seaside and country resorts. To increase manufacturing capacity a factory was built in Keighley to produce standard one colour back playing cards; by the end of the 1920s production reached 30,000 packs a week.

Waddingtons was also recognised as the foremost poster printers; during this period it produced the largest poster ever printed – it comprised twenty-four 60" x 40" sheets, which when pasted together measured 10 feet x 40 feet, and advertised the 1924 British Empire Exhibition. Each sheet contained an average of ten colours, nearly a million impressions being used in total, and the order consumed ten-and-a-half tons of paper and one-and-a-half tons of ink. However Waddingtons still retained their links with theatres, printing programmes for Moss Empires Ltd, a relationship which lasted for almost forty years. Other related work included a contract, which lasted for seven years, with the London Savoy Theatre, home at that time of the D'Oyly Carte Opera. In such work delivery date was sacred.

In the 1930s Victor Watson invested some of his own money in Satona Ltd, which made cartons using paper and paraffin wax to be supplied to dairies; it was a Danish idea. Victor Watson eventually became its chairman and Norman Watson became a director. Before the end of the Second World War the company was sold to Waddingtons and soon afterwards a container was developed for selling orange juice in cinemas.

In America the game of Monopoly was marketed by Parker Brothers, who in the early part of 1935 sent a sample to Waddingtons. Victor Watson asked his son Norman to look it over and tell him what he thought of the game. He played an imaginary game against himself, continuing through Friday night, Saturday night and Sunday night.

He was captivated. On the Monday morning he persuaded his father to telephone Parker Brothers; it was the first transatlantic telephone call Waddingtons had ever made. It resulted in Waddingtons being granted a licence to manufacture Monopoly. Only the name places and currency were changed, otherwise the rules were the same.

*Victor Watson in 1938;
below, a promotional
leaflet*

At the beginning of the war Waddingtons were asked to produce some low denomination bank notes, valued at 2s 6d and 5s, to replace coins. Security was very strict and very few people knew of their existence; they were never used but at the end of the war the government destroyed them. During the war Waddingtons and De La Rue had an agreement to help each other in cases of damage by enemy action. In 1940 De La Rue's London factory was gutted. Within days Waddingtons were printing foreign bank notes, and although not included in the agreement went on to print playing cards for both companies. On seeing the smouldering remains of the De La Rue factory Victor Watson, standing with the competitor's managing director, said: "For every pack of cards produced for John Waddington we shall manufacture one for De La Rue." It was a characteristic gesture!

In 1943 Waddingtons opened a small factory on the Team Valley Estate at Gateshead. That year was however to be a sad one for Waddingtons for it

saw the death of Victor Watson, the man who had done so much to ensure its success. Norman Watson and George Spink became joint managing directors. It was Norman Watson who organised for Picasso to supply a design for the back of a playing card, one used on the first plastic playing cards produced by Waddingtons. Norman's younger brother, Eric, also joined the firm and it was he who became involved in the project to sell a newly developed Easter Egg car-

The British Monopoly Championships in 1984

ton to Cadbury's; this led, for the first time, to the large scale sale of chocolate Easter Eggs.

During the 1950s a new subsidiary company was formed to sell games direct to retailers. The first game was 'Summit', and the subsidiary was called Summit Games, although this was later merged with the Games Section of the main company. Victor Watson jnr had now risen through the company and in 1956 was appointed assistant managing director. The following year Waddingtons made a further decisive move when, to accommodate the needs of Schweppes, it introduced vacuum formed plastic containers.

Valentine & Sons Ltd of Dundee, an old established greeting card company, was acquired in the 1960s. John Valentine had founded their company in 1826, producing wooden blocks for linen printing. In 1830 he was joined by his son, James, who introduced a pictorial envelope, the forerunner of the picture postcard, a product for which the firm became famous, along with Christmas cards and children's toy books.

Waddingtons already had a Business Forms Division but about this time a joint American company, Eureka Waddington, was formed in this country, primarily for the printing of trading stamps, the whole of the output being directed to the printing of Green Shield Stamps.

Subbuteo, the table soccer game, named after a falcon, Falco subbuteo, had been invented in 1947 by Peter Adolph, who lived in Kent, and in 1969 Subbuteo Sports Games Ltd was acquired by Waddingtons. In 1975 the Games Division was renamed Waddingtons House of Games Ltd. Victor Watson was now the guiding light in Waddingtons developments, and expansion was taking place at great speed.

In 1995, some years after the retirement of Victor Watson, the Games Division was sold to Hasbro, the American toy company, for £50 million. By now the sales of Waddington PLC were approximately £90 million of plastic containers in the USA, £100 million of folding cartons in the United Kingdom and Holland, other plastic packaging in the UK of £25 million and a fast-growing £70 million of printing for the financial services sector. In 1996 the name of the company was changed to Waddington PLC.

Cheese has been made in Wensleydale for at least 800 years, probably initially by the workers on estates, or 'granges', managed by the monks of the Cistercian Order, at monasteries such as Jervaulx. During the summer months the ewes would be milked twice a day and it was this sheep's milk which was turned into cheese.

The recipes for the making of cheese were probably brought by the monks from France, and for many years these were passed by word of mouth, or from watching other workers, from one generation to another. However this way of life was to change with the dissolution of the monasteries and from about the middle of the 17th century it was the cow, rather than the sheep, which was valued for its milk. The cow gave more milk and the period of lactation could be extended.

In those early days the farmer's wife did not have the modern advantages of a thermometer, and tested the heat of the milk by placing either the hand or the elbow in the vat; similarly she had no rennet, but she would take a small portion of the dried stomach of a young calf, known as 'keslop', boil it in a pan on the kitchen fire, strain off the liquid, and when cool, add it to the milk to cause it to coagulate. If she ran short of the keslop she would collect a black snail from a swamp and when this was submerged in the milk it had the same effect as the keslop. Early cheeses were pickled by salting them in brine, which not only gave the cheese flavour, but also cured it and gave it a unique texture and flavour.

Initially the cheeses would be either sold to the local grocer or offered to the corn merchant in exchange for the provisions needed for the farm and farmhouse. Some cheeses would also be sold at the annual cheese fair held each October in Yarm. Here cheese merchants gathered from many of the dales, to sell their cheeses to grocers and merchants who had travelled from urban areas to stock up with cheese for the Christmas season, traditionally a time when much cheese was eaten.

Edward Chapman, a Hawes corn and provision merchant, became one of Upper Wensleydale's largest buyers of farmhouse cheese. In 1897 he started to buy milk from those farms which had previously supplied him with poor quality cheese, in the belief that he could make better cheese than these farmers' wives. At least all the processes would be under his control, and if the cheese showed signs of not maturing properly he could sell it quickly. He started by buying about 200 gallons of milk a day and established the first factory to manufacture Wensleydale cheese, but it only operated in the summer months, closing for the winter. In Hawes there was also a woollen mill and when this also closed during that winter Edward Chapman bought it, converted it into a cheese factory and the next spring opened for business, taking in even more milk than before.

Meanwhile, Alfred Rowntree opened factories in the lower parts of the dale, at Masham, Coverham and Thoralby, collecting milk from Lower Wensleydale, Coverdale and Bishopdale.

Above, wrapping Wensleydale Cheese in a muslin cloth allows the flavour to develop as it matures; right, blocking, cutting and ripping

During the early years of the 20th century the bulk collection of milk by rail and wagon grew dramatically and cheese making declined. The ripe blue Wensleydale cheese became almost unobtainable, the public being persuaded to buy a white Wensleydale cheese which had not been allowed to mature. However Mr. Rowntree did produce a specialist factory-made mature Wensleydale blue which compared favourably with the farmhouse cheese.

The early 1930s were difficult years for many parts of Britain as the industrial depression set in, and the Wensleydale cheese producers struggled to keep going. There was no shortage of milk to process but there was over-production of cheese, and with cheeses being sent to Britain by our Colonies, prices plummeted. In 1933 the Milk Marketing Board was formed but the situation looked bleak for local cheese production when they offered farmers contracts which would take the Dales milk many miles away to a national dairy. However the farmers wanted the Hawes dairy to continue.

Kit Calvert, who has been described as 'the complete dalesman' with his clay pipe, windswept hair, and eyes full of life and humour, called a meeting in Hawes Town Hall in 1935 to rescue the dairy, the only one in the heart of Wensleydale producing cheese. With a capital of £1085, of which Kit Calvert had provided £200, some dales folk formed their own company and appointed Kit Calvert as their managing director. In 1936 'The Wensleydale Cheese Joint Conference' was formed, made up of three factory managers, three farmhouse cheesemakers, and four cheese factors, and this worked to improve the standard of the locally produced cheese and open new markets for their products. Before the Second World War tens of thousands of 1lb and 2lb 'smalls' were produced in November and December for the Christmas trade but for the duration of the war restrictions were imposed, and such specialist lines had to be withdrawn.

In 1953 Kit built a new £15,000 Wensleydale creamery in Hawes, and the same year re-introduced the 1lb 'Baby Wensleydale' cheese, which immediately became immensely popular, selling 50,000 in the first year; by the 1960s the figure had risen to 250,000 per year. Kit's initiative was proving a real success.

The Milk Marketing Board, realising its potential, purchased the Wensleydale Creamery, together with a dairy at Kirkby Malzeard, near Ripon, for £500,000, in 1966. The following year Kit, having reached the age of 65, decided to retire and devote more time to his interest in books, the Congregational Church, and his love of Wensleydale. In 1977 he was awarded the MBE. The Dale lost a great friend when Kit Calvert died in 1984, but his achievements still live on.

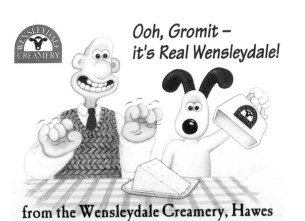

Ooh, Gromit – it's Real Wensleydale!

from the Wensleydale Creamery, Hawes

However in May 1992 disaster hit Wensleydale, and the whole of Yorkshire, when Dairy Crest, a subsidiary of the Milk Marketing Board, closed the Hawes creamery, the only one in the dale, and transferred production to Lancashire!

The 59 workers were devastated that their unique skills, gained over many years, were now being regarded as of no value, and many other people joined in the campaign to keep Wensleydale cheese making where it belonged. Kit Calvert would have been proud of them; Yorkshire folk were not going to accept a decision made by some anonymous conglomerate down in Surrey! The ex-managers took up the cause and in November 1992 a management buyout was finally agreed. On 16 December, with the help of a handful of the former workforce, cheesemaking in Wensleydale recommenced, in time for Christmas. The trial batches were a resounding success, Wensleydale cheese making was on its way up again.

The following year major refurbishment of the creamery took place, leading to an increase in the production of hand-made cheeses, and also in the number of local jobs. Real Wensleydale has to be hand-made and today the Wensleydale Creamery manufactures its quality cheeses, the traditional white and blue Wensleydale, as well as a range of more modern flavours which incorporate apricot, ginger, or fruit and nuts. Local cheese recipes are also now being rediscovered and gradually one or two are being added to the range.

Today at the creamery there is a viewing gallery so that visitors can see the whole of the cheese making process, and sample the cheese. But what is so special about Wensleydale cheese? To find out you must remove the traditional muslin cheesecloth, cut through the true rind, and then you will come to the creamy-white, flaky cheese which has a slightly honeyed aroma.

It isn't a solid block, as with some processed cheese, but crumbs will fall to the plate, just enough to excite the taste-buds. It is said that a piece of apple pie without Real Wensleydale is like a kiss without a squeeze. For me, Christmas cake, without my cheese, is just not complete!

WHITAKERS

Est. 1889

John Whitaker was one of the thirteen children of Wilson Whitaker who had farmed at Burnsall with his father William. John was born in 1857 at Birks Farm, Glusburn near Keighley. At an early age he went to Gargrave to work in his brother-in-law's grocery and drapery business. When he was about 25 he opened his first shop, trading as a grocer and draper in Cross Hills.

John and his wife Rebecca had two sons and a daughter, Ida who persuaded her father to turn his shop into a baker's and confectioner's, making the produce behind the shop, whilst the family lived above it. Ida was extremely talented, a woman of tenacity, no mean artist and deeply interested in music. Present members of the family stress that without her foundation there would be no business.

Ida started making chocolates in 1903. She

was taught by the wife of the Vicar of Kildwick. In about 1907 her brother Reg joined the firm, but any real expansion had to wait until after the First World War as he was called up to serve his country. In 1926 the business moved to a shop in Skipton High Street, where a restaurant was opened above it.

In 1934 Reg married Claire Smith, an employee. In 1940 the restaurant closed and Ida devoted her life to another business, 'The Treasure Galleries' in Skipton High Street. She died in 1957. After the war the family decided not to re-enter the restaurant business and since that time have leased their premises above the shop.

When Reg died in 1951 his wife Claire continued the business and spent most of the rest of her life running the family shop in the High Street, as well as overseeing the development of the embryonic chocolate manufactory on the site of an old bakery in Skipton.

Son John entered the business in 1955 but hated baking, believing it to be the way to nowhere, with low value goods, lack of productivity and poor shelf-life, not to mention limited sales in a small country town. His escape route, with the help and encouragement of his mother, and wife Anne, was to develop the potential of the small chocolate undertaking, where the chocolates were still made in the front room of a private house. His brother Fred worked with him, and together with loyal assistants Mrs Rissie Hawkins, Mrs Edith Varley and Ann Ryder who was secretary, gradually the business started to expand through sales to pubs, hotels, restaurants and shops.

In the late 1950s the era of the supermarkets was dawning and the future of the small independent bakery looked bleak. Bakery chains were developing and the age of the small crafts-

Whitaker's Skipton shop was converted from a private house and opened as a shop in October 1926

men was drawing to a close. In 1964 the family decided to expand the business and for the first time in the life of the firm they went to the bank to borrow big money! With the help of a benevolent building society manager and a very far seeing banker, Derek Sawyer, from York, the company found itself owing £250,000 and still hadn't sold another chocolate! It focused the mind – they decided that the route forward was to specialise and so selected a few of their best sellers and automated their production as far as possible.

One of the chocolates selected was a mint flavoured product derived from an old nougatine recipe used by Margery Smales, Claire's sister, who had previously worked with the company. Eventually this 'mint crisp', made on German machinery, became an international winner.

Whitakers Restaurant
HIGH STREET   SKIPTON
Open 7 days 9 a.m. to 6 p.m.
OUTSIDE CATERING & HIRE SERVICE
A.A. Approved   Tel. 3750

An advertisement from Dalesman, 1965 in stark comparison to today's sophisticated image below

Sadly, the introduction of mechanisation has resulted in the loss of old time favourites which can't be produced in this way. However, with the help of Peter, Claire's youngest son, an engineer, it became possible to maximise the efficiency of the machinery the company has to rely on, including the temperature controlled storage facilities, which are used to ensure Whitakers' chocolates reach the outlet in peak condition.

Winning new outlets is always difficult, but Whitakers have a way that at the time was unique. Chocolates are taken to hotels, restaurants and other possible customers by totally independent distributors who have found gaps in the market; the late Joan and Teddy Gifford secured a particular niche for the company's 'After Dinner Mints'.

William Whitaker, John's eldest son – a fourth generation chocolatier, went 'on the road' as such a distributor before joining the management team and is now managing director. James, John's youngest son, is better known as captain of Leicestershire County Cricket Club, whilst John's daughter, Sally, now runs the refurbished Whitaker's shop, a separate company, in the

High Street, renamed after Claire in appreciation of her part in the company's development. Today with John Whitaker as chairman, William Whitaker as managing director and Joan Huck as general manager the firm is establishing itself world-wide as suppliers of quality chocolates. Their products go to 25 countries, with Scandinavia being to the forefront.

On the wrappers is a candelabra with three lighted candles, an idea conceived from the piano of Liberace; and three candles in a candelabra form a 'W' for Whitakers. Three candles could also represent the three generations who have shone and shown us how to spoil ourselves, and our loved ones, with perfect chocolates.

Whiteley & Green Ltd

In 1879 an agreement was drawn up between cousins Henry Whiteley of Mount Pleasant, Holmfirth and Hurst Green of Scholecroft, near Holmfirth. It stated that the two partners would carry on business together as woollen cloth manufacturers at Hinchliffe Mill, near Holmfirth, and that each of the partners 'shall be allowed a salary of thirty shillings per week for his services out of the said partnership business.' At first they could only lease the four-storey mill which was powered by a water-wheel, but later they bought it. In those early days their speciality was Bedford cord.

Hurst Green had no family but Henry Whiteley had four sons and at various times they all worked for the firm. Tragically the mill was extensively damaged by fire in 1901 but during the following year it was restored, this time as a three-storey building, although at the same time new buildings were added to house the weaving, mending, scouring and dyeing departments.

Also in 1902 the firm became a limited liability company.

The early years of the 20th century were not easy ones for the company. One of Henry Whiteley's sons died at the early age of 37, and in 1914 Hurst Green died while only 57 years old. After Hurst Green's death the Whiteley family negotiated to take over control of the company.

1914 also saw the death of the company's other founder, Henry Whiteley, at the age of 73 years. This period of the First World War was a busy time as the company worked night and day to produce Khaki Bedford Cord for the mounted artillery, and to supply riding material to Egypt and South Africa.

By 1922 all the mill's machinery was run by steam power; this was the period when Whiteley & Green first introduced their Cavalry Twill. The weaves produce cloth of fine face appearance, but which can be a very heavy cloth if required; it became very popular at this time. The early death of members of the Whiteley family was a real loss, two other sons of the founder dying in four years, one aged 54, the other at the early age of 43. In 1930 Henry Whiteley's only remaining son, Charles Henry Whiteley, became sole managing director, but he died in 1939. Once again the country was at war with Germany and although third generation members of the family had now entered the business they were called away to the armed forces. During the war the firm was managed by the widow of the late managing director, C. H. Whiteley, Mrs. F. Whiteley, and the firm's solicitor, the firm's accountant, and Hubert Marsh, the secretary.

Just before the end of the war, in 1944,

Early days: Henry Whiteley (seated) among the workers in the finishing department in 1910 an extremely heavy cloud-burst over the Holme Valley caused disastrous flooding of the river which totally destroyed the mill's finishing room. As the company recovered from the war years they introduced new automatic weaving machinery and converted away from steam power to electricity. Now a new finishing room was built and new facilities were created to house warping and winding departments.

The 1960s were good years for the industry and Whiteley & Green continued their modernisation policy to ensure they kept to the forefront, especially in the production of Cavalry Twill, for which they had long had a worldwide reputation. In 1966 the mill was the first in the Huddersfield area to introduce double-day shift working.

As the company moved towards its centenary, advances in applied technology meant that once again the directors must upgrade their facilities, and in 1971 new Rapier looms were acquired for the weaving department and the scouring department was re-equipped. To meet demand, and to exploit the value of the new expensive machinery, night shifts were introduced in 1973. New techniques were introduced in 1977 with the installation of ring spinning machinery.

What should have been a joyous occasion in 1979, the firm's centenary, was clouded as the textile industry had to face up to a deepening trade recession. For Whiteley & Green this meant that the firm must change direction and so they decided to start manufacturing fancy woollens.

Computerisation came to the company in 1981; the following year they gained their first export order to Japan. Having taken major steps to ensure they had the best in machinery, now was the time to ensure that their designs met customer demands and therefore they appointed a chief designer, also developing a new design studio and showroom.

In recent years further high speed weaving machines have been added and today all production planning is fully computerised. Whiteley &

The modern spinning section

Green may be based in a remote corner of the Yorkshire uplands but their cloth is to be found in all parts of Europe as well as in the United States, Canada, South Africa, Hong Kong and Singapore. The uses of their cloths are extremely wide, ranging from high quality jacketings and sports suitings, to cloths used in upholstery and others even in industrial filters.

Whiteley & Green are still renowned for their world-famed Cavalry Twill and also for their Bedford cords, cloths they have made from their earliest days, now incorporating much lighter weights of fabric as required by modern fashion.

J. WOOD & SONS LTD
Established 1850

Joe Wood was born in Halifax on 12 July 1826, the son of a musician who had been a trumpeter in the band of the Royal Horse Guards Blue Regiment. When Joe's father left the army he and his wife settled in Huddersfield, where she had inherited some property. Joe's father pulled down the old house and rebuilt the premises to include a large room which was used for concerts and operatic performances. Joe was therefore brought up in an atmosphere of music and as he grew up his love of music developed.

At the age of three or four he learned to play the French horn, and later the trumpet. When another child prodigy visited Huddersfield it was suggested that Master Joe and this other young chap should play a duet. However Joe had to prove, at the age of six, that he could blow top C on his instrument and and he was actually brought from his bed to prove the point. Needless to say he succeeded and afterwards played the duet!

He joined the Huddersfield Old Band, of which his father was the bandmaster, and played the triangle. At the age of seven Joe began to play the piano and was taught by Mr. Henry Horn, the organist at St. Paul's Church, who also conducted the Huddersfield Choral Society. When he was 13 years old he was appointed organist of the Methodist New Connexion Church in High Street, being chosen from 13 candidates; he held the post for 13 years before becoming organist and choirmaster at St. Paul's Church, a position he held for over 20 years. He also played the violin in the orchestra of the Huddersfield Choral Society.

Joe Wood became a teacher of both the piano and singing. In 1850, aged 24, he started in business as a dealer in pianos, other musical instruments and seller of sheet music in Huddersfield's John William Street, and later moved to premises near to the Lion Arcade. The firm became Wood & Marshall, after Joshua Marshall became his brother-in-law. About ten years after opening the shop he started to manufacture pianos at premises in Fitzwilliam Street. His early pianos had wooden frames, crude mechanisms and

Centre, Joe Wood; left a concert ensemble of 1855 arranged by Joe Wood (left to right, Miss Newbould, Mrs Sunderland, Mr Ingersolm Mr Henry Phillips and Joe Wood

stood five feet tall; however they were often used by leading artists of the day. Apparently his mother attended to the customers in the shop while he gave organ, piano and singing lessons in a back room. About 1870, to meet public taste for something more refined, he produced the piccolo piano, which was only three feet high and was much favoured by the ladies, who at that time wore long skirts.

Joe Wood married Sarah and they had six sons and four daughters. He was a zealous Freemason.

In about 1877 Joe sent his son, William Henry Wood, to open another shop in New Ivegate, Bradford, where he took over an already established music business. Around 1882 the Huddersfield part of the business was moved to new premises in New Street which they aptly named Beethoven House. As public demand increased for more elaborate pianos, such as the grand piano and table grand piano, Joe decided to give up making pianos and started selling the new Edison gramophone with its cylindrical records.

Wood's became synonymous with musical entertainment in Bradford. They organised the first visit of the Halle Orchestra to the city, when it was reported that "Mr. Halle barely

A letterhead from the late 1800s; right, a Rosewood piano guarantee from 1914; below, Wood's exhibition stand from the 1920s

escaped an encore". Sometimes, as on the occasion of the visit of Vladimar de Pachmann, a Russian pianist, the audience was small and the admission charges did not meet the fee, but this was part of Joe's generosity to the musical life of Bradford. Towards the end of his life he received many acknowledgements of his outstanding contribution to the area. Joe Wood died in 1884 aged 57; he was remembered by many as a well loved and respected employer and friend. After Joe's death the partnership with Joshua Marshall ceased, and only members of the Wood family have carried the business forward.

The firm became J Wood & Sons in 1902. In 1905 a serious fire destroyed the New Ivegate shop and they moved to the Mechanics Institute before taking premises in Sunbridge Road in 1911, which they occupied for the next 60 years. Joe's son, Percy, who was later to handle all the firm's musical promotions, began his musical career at the age of 11 when he became a pianist in the St George's Hall orchestra in Bradford. Joe's other sons, Charles and Harold Wood, also joined the business.

Radio and records later became a major part of their trade but they still specialised in piano restoration, repairing and tuning as well as keeping an extensive selection of sheet music of all types. From the 1950s television was also to become an important aspect of their work.

In 1964 the Huddersfield store was completely destroyed by fire, but within a weekend the shop had re-opened in temporary premises, and they then rebuilt to provide appropriate premises for each of the different aspects of the business. At this time the electronic organ became central to the firm's activities, both for home and church use. In 1967 a shop was opened in Wakefield, and Gough & Davy of Hull is now part of the company.

Today the business operates as two separate companies. J Wood & Sons Ltd retain the Bradford and Hull premises, under the chairmanship of Joe Wood's great, great grandson, Richard Wood. The flagship operation at Bradford, reputedly the largest music shop in the country, has a vast selection of pianos, organs, sheet music and classical CDs.

Following the tradition of the founder it houses one of the best equipped piano workshops in the country. It is also home to the world renowned Early Music Shop (with a branch in London), manufacturing early musical instruments and supplying them to every part of the globe, and the Bradford Computing Organ Company, well known for its production of pipeless church organs.

The Huddersfield and Wakefield shops are now owned by R E Wood, who has recently formed his own firm.

WOODS

George Woods worked for Castle Mills in Knaresborough. At that time there were many who worked in the flax mills as flax dressers, commonly referred to as 'hecklers', but it is thought that George was either a salesman for or a manager at the mill; Castle Mills made glass cloths for the royal households. In the 1830s about 2000 people were employed in the linen industry in the town, and the whole of Nidderdale was famous for its linen weaving and bleaching.

George's son, William Ernest Woods, was born in Knaresborough and he followed in his father's footsteps, but also undertook a three year apprenticeship with Marshall & Snelgrove in Leeds before opening his own shop in 1895 in

Harrogate's Princes Street, now Princes Square. Even in those days prior to the First World War he was regularly supplying the town's major hotels and it was not unusual to see the staff pushing a handcart piled high with quality linens and towels. In his early days he would personally dress the shop window in the morning, before cycling off to Knaresborough to purchase items from the mill. Such were his standards of business he would not even sell a dishcloth unless it was the best and sure to give good service. Soon he had a reputation which extended across the whole of Britain. When Princess Mary, later Princess Royal, came to live at Harewood, Woods gained royal patronage, and throughout the years have supplied many of Britain's prestigious homes.

Unfortunately William Woods had an accident while riding his motorcycle, trying to avoid a carriage and pair as it pulled out of a driveway, and for the rest of his life he had to walk with the aid of a stick. This however did not stop him sliding down the bannister at the shop, much to the surprise of unsuspecting staff! During the First World War, being unable to join the forces, he converted his own home into a soup kitchen, also providing dinners and teas for locally based troops. In many ways William was a retiring man but was a keen worker for the Wesley Methodist Church in Harr-

Left the Princes Street shop; centre William Woods in a buying visit to the Belfast Linen Manufacturers just after the First World war

Two posters from the 1930s

ogate, being a local preacher and bible class leader. He had a never failing sense of humour, was always willing to give sound advice and in an unobtrusive way was generous to many who found themselves in need.

At the end of the First World War, Woods offered brides of the 'roaring '20s' a trousseau of table, bed, bathroom and kitchen linens at a cost of £11. "Though modest in cost, every item has been carefully selected for reliability in wear," wrote Mr Woods in his advertisement.

The business was later transferred to Station Parade, into the premises used today. William had two sons and on his death in 1940 George chose to run the business whilst his brother William E (Ernest) became a senior partner in a local firm of solicitors. George showed many of the concerns of the founder, for when one of the staff, James Lambert, went to serve in the Second World War he received letters each week from his employer. Mr Lambert returned to Woods after the war and eventually completed 64 years service with the firm!

Tragedy came to the firm in 1965 when George Woods and his wife, Thalia, were both killed in a motor accident as they were on their way to Ireland to visit one of their suppliers. At that time William, George's son, and grandson of the founder, was only 17 and had intended following his uncle in a career in law, but hurriedly had to make a decision to leave school and enter the business, or allow the business to be sold.

When he entered the business he knew nothing about it, nor did he enjoy it, indeed he hated it! However he had to start with the basic skills, learning to wrap parcels correctly, using brown paper and string. Under the guidance of his uncle he was soon sent to Northern Ireland, to the home of linen, to learn about the fabric in all its conditions. After this it was a spell at Heal's in London and then a course in interior-design before coming home to Harrogate again. Over succeeding years he took every opportunity to travel to the Far East, India, America, and other parts of Europe, in each country meeting designers and manufacturers, creating direct links so that he could buy direct new and exciting merchandise for the shop.

As the business grew William purchased the adjoining shop and also developed the company's interior design service. This latter part of the business now undertakes work for homes all over the United Kingdom and sometimes overseas. Still they supply monogrammed linen sheets or hand embroidered pillow cases – they are proud of their heritage, but are always looking to the future.

THE WYEDEAN WEAVING COMPANY LIMITED

The story of Wyedean starts far from Yorkshire, in Coventry, on the 25th November 1851, Robert Arnold Dalton and George Samuel Barton entered into partnership as ribbon manufacturers.

Robert Dalton was born in 1825 and by the age of 14 had started a seven-year apprenticeship with William and John Sargent, who were ribbon makers in Coventry. In 1847 he became a ribbon manufacturer and later in life was elected an alderman and mayor of the city. We know little of his partner George Barton except that he was probably a year younger than Robert.

During the latter half of the 19th century many ribbon pictures of royalty and sporting scenes were created in Coventry and those woven by Dalton and Barton are among the best known.

The partnership extended from ribbon making to the manufacture of coach lace and upholstery trimmings, but in 1872 it became a limited company. At this time two of their staff, Thomas Moy Hammerton and Edward Turrall took over production, with the exception of the ribbon making which the original partners retained. Dalton Barton & Co had premises in Aldersgate Street, London, which became their registered office, and at White Friars Lane and Monk Park Street in Coventry.

Much of the narrow ribbon trade became mechanised. A great boost for the company came when they won orders to supply the newly formed Australian railways with tape to join the moquette seat covering.

St. Nicholas's Church in King Street, Coventry, was demolished and a factory built in the 1870s. Both Robert Dalton and George Barton were churchgoers and they felt this was the ideal site to build their factory. A new factory was built in Mason Road, Coventry in the 1940s.

David Wright, with a background in textile design, joined the company in 1959; he had no experience in narrow fabrics. He was chosen to introduce young blood to the company, to take a hard look at the firm, and to move the business away from Coventry as it was proving increasingly difficult to compete for labour with the booming motor industry. David discovered that it had been their policy to weave anything

Left, the Haworth mills; above, a wall hanging tapestry by Dalton Barton

THE BRIDGEHOUSE MILLS CO. LTD.

WORSTED COATING MANUFACTURERS. **HAWORTH.**

they were asked to do, but this meant that many machines only ran for a few weeks a year. Mr. Barton's son-in-law who lived in the Forest of Dean found a suitable factory at nearby Coleford. The work was rationalised and the move was made. This element of the company now needed a new name and David suggested, due to its location, "Wyedean".

Dalton Barton & Co Ltd had become one of the largest haberdashery suppliers in the world and now they felt was the time to sell off this narrow fabric division as it did not fit into their main business area. In 1964 David Wright struck a deal with the owners that he would dispose of everything and oversee the closedown if he could have the military part of the business, making officer ranking braid, sashes, chevron lace, parachute harnessess etc and puttee tapes. He looked around the Coleford area for a suitable building in which to locate this work but on finding nothing suitable he returned to his native Haworth, in West Yorkshire, and in an old textile mill found a room to rent.

Soon he and his wife, Norma, were in business; he was weaving and she was sewing. Gradually the business grew, some staff being employed in Bridgehouse Mill whilst others helped as outworkers. In 1971 he bought the premises of the Bridgehouse Spinning Co. but was only able to afford part of the building. Shortly afterwards a firm of braid cord commission workers in Bury who owed David Wright some money agreed that he take over the company. Machinery was brought to Haworth and once again the range of products was expanded – it may not be generally recognised that many army ties are braided, not woven – this would form an important part of their military specialism.

Today Wyedean, still with its mix of factory-workers and outworkers, employs 80 people who make a vast array of military accoutrements ranging from rank insignia, trouser striping, chevrons, epaulettes and cap bands for the armed forces of countries which were previously part of the British Empire. When the Guards are on parade at the trooping of the colour probably all their uniform accessories, the adornments to their swords or musical instruments, will have been made in Haworth. Prestigious and novel items from false eyebrows for camels (Royal Jordanian Army cavalry mosquito repellents) to sashes worn by the Queen; from American Civil War regimental laces to slow match cord for firing a 21-gun salute; all contribute to the lifeblood of Wyedean Weaving.

Still their largest customer is the Ministry of Defence, but other supplies go to military tailors, theatrical costumiers and to clothe staff of some of the world's top hotels.

YORKSHIRE POST

Griffith Wright, who was born about 1733, and whose father was the clerk at St John's Church in Briggate, Leeds, was really the founder of the Yorkshire Post, a newspaper with a national and international reputation. The paper's first home was in Lowerhead Row but the following year, 1755, it moved to New Street End. Also in 1755 Griffith married Mary Pullen, and later they had a son Thomas.

In the mid 1700s Leeds was emerging as a busy market town for the woollen trade; it was also a time of social change, and Wright's weekly newspaper, the Leeds Intelligencer, recorded the happenings of his day. The first issue was published on 2 July 1754, but as today it was not a monopoly situation, for Griffith had to compete with the Leeds Mercury, which had been started by John Hirst in 1718. Griffith set out as his aims: "Whatever may usefully Instruct, or innocently Amuse the Reader, will be suitable Matter of Intelligence for this Paper."

The first paper had four pages, of three columns, each filled with a mix of news from the London journals, and advertisements, among them ones for patent medicines, sold by the proprietors. It originally cost about 2d, although no price appeared on it; newspapers were taxed by the government, and as the tax increased so the cost of the newspaper increased, to 3d in 1777, and to 4d in 1793. Advertisements were also subject to duty, but being a true blue paper the Intelligencer did not complain, for indeed some of its advertisements would be of a political nature.

Griffith edited his own paper for over 30 years, before he handed over to his son in 1785. Thomas was editor until he died in 1805, being outlived by his father, and his son, also Griffith Wright, succeeded him. Apparently Griffith Jnr. was a man of wit with a 'sarcastic pen', but was also a very competent editor.

The 1807 Yorkshire election was fought mainly on industrial concerns, the candidates being William Wilberforce, Lord Milton [Whig], and Lord Lascelles [Tory]. The Intelligencer took the unpopular side by supporting the Tory, who lost, but this decision was reversed at the next election when Lord Lascelles' support for the future of the new, larger manufacturers was seen to be the way forward for the country.

In 1809 the title of the paper changed to Wright's Leeds Intelligencer, to compete with the Mercury. In March 1811 the first full 'Supplement' came out; the following year they introduced a new and larger type, and in 1813

they installed a Stanhope press which cost £50 – machine production was still a long way off!

It wasn't until March 1817 that a 'Second Edition' is mentioned, published occasionally to cover news of the Manchester riots. At this time 'leading articles' were unknown, although Parliamentary reports had appeared as early as 1785. The paper carried no illustrations and much of the editorial work still involved 'scissors-and-paste'.

In 1815 George Mudie came as editor of the Intelligencer, but when Wright sold the paper in

THE YORKSHIRE POST. WEDNESDAY, AUGUST 5. 1914.

ENGLAND DECLARES WAR AGAINST GERMANY.

BRITISH ULTIMATUM REJECTED.

ARMY AND NAVY MOBILISED.

TERRITORIALS EMBODIED.

BRITISH RAILWAYS UNDER STATE CONTROL.

1818 Mudie violated the sale agreement, and started the Leeds Independent in partnership with William Headley. When Mudie was editor of the Intelligencer it made a profit of £1000 a year; after he left, profits fell to £100 for a time, but in the end the Intelligencer absorbed the Independent in 1826.

Griffith Wright Snr. died in 1818 and soon after this his grandson sold the paper and developed interests in other directions, including becoming Mayor of Leeds in 1834/5.

In 1819 the paper was taken over by Gawtress & Co, who changed its title to The Leeds Intelligencer and Yorkshire General Advertiser and in 1822 it was sold to Joseph Ogle Robinson and John Hernaman. Robinson came from an old Leeds family which had had close connections with the Leeds Library from its beginnings in 1768. The Library had moved to Commercial Street, and now the Intelligencer moved to the same premises; Commercial Street was to be the paper's home for the rest of its days. John Hernaman was a good newspaperman who saw the paper through two

very difficult years, 1828-1829, and remained in charge until 1832 when they appointed 25 year old Alaric Watts as editor.

Although in the early days the paper was available in London, as well as in parts of Yorkshire and Lancashire, the coach to London could take up to three days. By 1836, when coaching days were coming to an end, this time had dropped to about 23 hours, although delays due to accidents, etc. were still frequent.

In 1866 the Intelligencer became a daily paper. A newly formed company, the Yorkshire Conservative Newspaper Co Ltd, turned the Intelligencer into the Yorkshire Post, but it wasn't until 1923 that they were able to acquire the Leeds Mercury; the two papers continued as separate publications, strong rivals from the same stable. With the coming of the Second World War, and the resultant shortage of newsprint, the two papers merged under the editorship of William Linton Andrews, who in 1954 was knighted for his outstanding work on the paper.

The Yorkshire Evening Post was introduced in 1890, eventually absorbing its rival, the Yorkshire Evening News, in 1963. In 1967 the company, under the title Yorkshire Post Newspapers Ltd, merged with United Newspapers Ltd.

That year they acquired a site alongside the River Aire, opening their new headquarters in 1970. The £5million project provided the largest hybrid press installation in the world, combining web offset with simultaneous traditional letterpress processes.

Today new offset presses use the equivalent of 123,750 miles of paper and 311 tonnes of ink each year to print the Yorkshire Post. The presses are rooted onto the floor, standing on piles sunk 30 feet into the ground. Newspapers have come a long way from those with no illustrations to today's which carry many pictures, a large number being in full colour. As we approach a new millennium the Yorkshire Post

The Yorkshire Post headquarters in Leeds, built in 1970, cost £5million

has a daily circulation of 78,000; every day it also has a specialised supplement. No longer does the paper go to the capital by stage coach, but by train and plane it quickly reaches many parts of the world bringing regional, national and international news, not only to home-sick 'Tykes', but to many others who respect its journalistic quality. Now, on line to the new millennium, the Yorkshire Post appears each day on the Internet, as Yorkshire Post Interactive, so that anywhere in the world the paper can be read on its day of issue.